# WHERE TO GO
# WHAT TO DO
# IN SCOTLAND

*500 places to visit in the
WET and DRY*

by
## MALCOLM A. SCOTT

Regional editorial and sales manager, Malcolm Scott

Illustrations by Robert Frost

Published by Heritage Publications,
Merchants House, Barley Market Street,
Tavistock, Devon

in association with

## NEW ENGLISH LIBRARY
TIMES MIRROR

Cover: Edinburgh Castle and Ben Nevis from across
Loch Linnhe

I.S.B.N. 0 903975 77 7

First edition February 1979
Second edition February 1980

Printed in Great Britain by William Collins Sons & Co., Ltd.

# FOREWORD

Since the first "Where to go What to do" guide appeared just 10 years ago nearly half a million copies of the series have been sold. Gradually the editions have been expanded to cover about half of England and the whole of Scotland with further titles in the pipeline.

In the autumn of each year the editorial team carries out the mammoth task of checking every single entry. Their own personal knowledge from visits during the summer is supplemented through a vast mailout to virtually every tourist attraction seeking details of opening times and further amendments for the following year.

All this checking means that we can publish a series of "Where to go What to do" guides which are truly all-year, all-weather, all-family, all-purpose publications.

**All-year** through the use of a "W" symbol to identify places which are open throughout the year. About a third of all tourist trips in the U.K. by car are taken between October and March and that means some 26 million trips out of an annual total of about 80 million — more tourist attractions might do well to note these statistics and cater for the winter tripper.

**All-weather** through the use of the umbrella symbol to pick out those places which provide shelter on the all too frequent days in our climate when clouds bring along the rain.

**All-family** through the symbol for children which identifies the attractions particularly suitable for youngsters and through the basic facts about all the places which can be read before setting out to select the one which will match the mood or wishes of those taking a trip whatever their interests or age group.

**All-purpose** because the wide variety of places included enables each guide to be used to plan day trips from home, long weekends away, or holidays of a week or more, either touring or making day trips while on vacation. At the top of each entry are the mileages and road numbers to neighbouring towns to assist identification of locations. At the bottom are the "See also" references to other places nearby which can be looked up so that the reader can determine which is likely to be of most interest to him or her before driving there.

And all this means that the guides help to save expensive petrol and repay their purchase price many times over. How many other product these days help you to enjoy yourself and save money?!

Know where to go and what to do through this series of guides.

# SCOTLAND — THE COUNTRY

Wild, rugged, majestic, alluring, romantic, enchanting . . . these are but some of the highly descriptive adjectives which have been used time without number to describe the type of scenery found in the vast 29,795 sq. miles that comprises Scotland (slightly over half the combined area of England and Wales). Yet none of these, let it be said, has ever been abused or even over-dramatised in its context for here, indeed, we have a land mass, interspersed with a myriad of lochs and lochans, which freely lends itself to such complimentary, if somewhat contradictory, terms.

Historically, Scotland has had more than its fair share of turmoil through the ages. Wars, feuds and uprisings plagued the country for many centuries leaving in their wake a wealth of castles, abbeys, churches and other buildings, many now but fragmentary ruins bearing witness to crimes most heinous. Suppression by wealthy landowners gave rise to embitterment on the part of crofters and generations were to pass before the situation became tenable far less totally resolved.

Scotland, unlike England and Wales (more especially the former), is for its size, bereft of population, its mere 5¼ m. being scarcely 1/5th of the rest of Great Britain. So, too, from an economic standpoint the country can never hope to be a European force in the truest sense of the phrase. But times are changing and changing rapidly. Gone are the days when Scotland was a subserviant nation to London's Westminster.

North Sea oil and its resultant huge potential of wealth to the entire country is in top gear and great cities like Aberdeen, the once uncharted wastes around Kishorn in Wester Ross and the hitherto remote Shetlands are prospering, or about to prosper, almost beyond credibility. The land of the 'mountain and the flood' is in a transitional stage — a stage which is quickly making it a land of oil and money.

## HOW TO GET THERE

**BY TRAIN:** British Rail operate a wide range of through day and overnight trains to Edinburgh and Glasgow from principal cities in England. There are also through trains to Perth, Fort William and Aberdeen. Excellent connecting facilities exist when no through trains are available. Principal routes and services are as follows:

London — Peterborough — York — Newcastle — Edinburgh (day or night)
London — West Midlands — Crewe — Preston — Glasgow/ Edinburgh (day or night)

London — East Coast — Edinburgh — Fort William (overnight only)

London — West Midlands — Preston — Perth — Inverness (day or night)

London — East Coast — Edinburgh — Dundee — Aberdeen (day or night)

**BY COACH.** The Scottish Bus Group and National Travel operate many express coach services between England and Scotland. Advance booking is essential. Principal services include:

London — Edinburgh/Glasgow/Aberdeen/Fife.

Manchester/Liverpool — Carlisle — Glasgow/Edinburgh.

Hull — Newcastle — Edinburgh — Glasgow.

Coventry/Birmingham — Carlisle — Glasgow.

Leicester/Nottingham — Carlisle — Glasgow/Edinburgh.

**BY AIR.** Direct flights connect Glasgow with Belfast, Birmingham, East Midlands, Leeds, Liverpool, London (Heathrow), London (Gatwick), Luton, Manchester, Newcastle.

To Edinburgh there are direct flights from Belfast, Birmingham, London (Heathrow), London (Gatwick), Norwich and Teesside.

A range of direct and connecting flights link Inverness and Aberdeen with London. Connections for Islay, Campbeltown, Tiree, Barra, Uist, Stornoway, Wick, Orkney and Shetland are available at Glasgow, Inverness and Aberdeen.

# DRIVING

Scotland, unlike parts of England (especially the West Country), has no great traffic problem even in the busiest months of July and August. Certainly the country's main arteries with the South, the A74/M74 Carlisle to Glasgow and the A1 (Great North Road) from Newcastle-upon-Tyne to Edinburgh can be extremely busy at these peak periods. Further north the main routes to the Highlands (A82 from Glasgow to Inverness via Loch Lomondside, Glencoe and Fort William) and the M9/A9 Edinburgh to Inverness via Stirling, Perth, Pitlochry and Aviemore carry the bulk of holiday traffic and delays can be expected on narrow, twisting stretches such as are encountered along most of Loch Lomond. In the main, however, long tailbacks are fortunately few and far between. Motorists from the South should note that, in many Highland areas apart from the routes mentioned, 'A' category roads are provided with 'passing places' where, basically, the unwritten rule is for drivers to pull into one of these depending on whether their car or the one approaching is nearest the inshot. Scotland is well served by

# Scotland - so much to see

*Falkland Palace*

... and you can see the best of Scotland for only £5.

The Royal Palace at Falkland, with its memories of Mary Queen of Scots. Glenfinnan Monument, where the Jacobite '45 Rising started. Culloden, where it ended bloodily a year later in the last land battle on British soil. Craigievar Castle, which stands today virtually as the masons left it in 1626. Inverewe gardens famed for the South Pacific and Himalayan plants flourishing incredibly on the same latitude as Leningrad. Glen Coe, with its grim memories of the massacre of 1692. The spot on Bannockburn battlefield where King Robert the Bruce is said to have unfurled his battle standard in 1314. Souter Johnnie's Cottage, the home of the Kirkoswald village cobbler, forever immortalised in Burns' "Tam o' Shanter".

All priceless parts of Scotland's heritage–cared for and maintained by the National Trust for Scotland. For your £5 annual membership you can visit these–and a further 80 properties, and over 80,000 acres open to the public–without further charge.

**The National Trust for Scotland is not, as many people think, a government department. It is a charity, and as such relies solely on its members and supporters to continue its aims of promoting Scotland. Why not become a member?**
You can enrol at many of our properties–or fill in the coupon.

 **THE NATIONAL TRUST FOR SCOTLAND**
5 Charlotte Square Edinburgh EH2 4DU   031-226 5922

7

secondary roads which often have good surfaces and particularly light traffic. To know these roads, and the scores of others which reach to the quiet little villages 'off the beaten track', a good motoring map is essential. The following are to be recommended. Ordnance Survey, Routemaster Series of Great Britain: (Sheets 1-4). 1 Orkney, Shetland and Western Islands, 2 Northern Scotland, 3 Western Central Scotland, 4 Central Scotland and Northumberland (all quarter-inch to 1 mile). Alternatively, AA 3 miles to 1 inch Touring Maps by "Geographia" cover the entire country in 10 sheets viz. 18 South-West Scotland, 19 Glasgow and Clyde, 20 Edinburgh and Glasgow, 21 Oban and Fort William, 22 Perth and Dundee, 23 Inverness and Skye, 24 Aberdeen and Inverness, 25 Skye and Outer Hebrides, 26 North Scotland, 27 Orkney and Shetland.

The Head Offices of motoring organisations in Scotland are: **Automobile Association**, Fanum House, Erskine Harbour, Erskine, Renfrewshire. (041) 812 0144. **Royal Automobile Club**, 242 West George St., Glasgow. (041) 248 4444.


# WEATHER

There's no getting away from the fact that Scotland's weather can be extremely unpredictable and varied from one part of the country to another. Unfortunately, some of the finest scenic areas are subject to the heaviest rainfall and figures prove that July and August, the peak summer months, are decidedly wetter, in almost the whole of Scotland, than June and September. Albeit, there are several parts of the country which experience drier weather over a 12 month period than, for instance, does London, Torquay and Penzance. The recognised 'dry areas' of Scotland are, in descending order, Dunbar (Lothian), Lossiemouth (Grampian), Arbroath (Tayside), Edinburgh (Lothian), Inverness (Highland) and St. Andrews (Fife).

Over a full year the country's sunniest areas have consistently proved to be Dunbar (Lothian), Arbroath (Tayside), St. Andrews (Fife) and Tiree (Strathclyde) in that order though even the leader of these, Dunbar with 1514.9 hrs., bears no match for England's S. coast resorts e.g. Torquay (1760 hrs.) and Bournemouth (1746 hrs.). One major plus factor in Scotland's favour is, however, its long hours of daylight during the early summer months (May, June and July). On the longest day (June 22), there is no complete darkness in northern Scotland and in, say Aberdeen and Inverness, you can manage a whole round of golf in the late evening when only the first couple of holes could be played around London during the same period.

Weather phone numbers are listed under the cities and towns

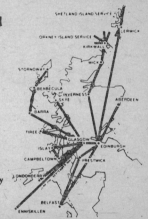

9

where the G.P.O. provides a service. Below, for your convenience, are the numbers of the places included in Scotland.

Edinburgh   (031) 246 8091
Glasgow    (041) 246 8091
Dundee     (038 34) 2566
Aberdeen   (0224) 722331.

## USEFUL ADDRESSES

**British Airways,** 85 Buchanan St., Glasgow. (041) 332 9666
135 Princes St., Edinburgh. (031) 225 2525
**British Railways (Scottish Board),** Buchanan House, 58 Port Dundas Rd., Glasgow. (041) 332 9811; (041) 221 3223.
**Caledonian MacBrayne Ltd.,** The Pier, Gourock, Renfrewshire. (0475) 33755.
**Department of the Environment,** Argyle House, 3 Lady Lawson St., Edinburgh. (031) 229 9191.
**Forestry Commission,** 231 Corstorphine Rd., Edinburgh. (031) 334 0303.
**Highlands and Islands Development Board,** Bridge House, 27 Bank St., Inverness. (0463) 34171.
**Loganair Ltd.,** St. Andrew's Drive, Glasgow Airport, Paisley. (041) 889 3181.
**National Trust for Scotland,** 5 Charlotte Square, Edinburgh. (031) 226 5922.
**Nature Conservancy,** 12 Hope Terrace, Edinburgh. (031) 447 4784.
**North of Scotland, Orkney and Shetland Shipping Co. (P. & O. Ferries),** Matthew's Quay, Aberdeen. (0224) 572615; (085 685) 655.
**Royal Society for the Protection of Birds,** 17 Regent Terrace, Edinburgh. (031) 556 5624.
**Scottish Bus Group,** 114 George St., Edinburgh. (031) 226 7491.
**Scottish Civic Trust,** 24 George Square, Glasgow (041) 221 1466.
**Scottish Sports Council,** 1 St. Colme St., Edinburgh. (031) 225 8411.
**Scottish Tourist Board,** 23 Ravelston Terrace, Edinburgh. (031) 332 2433. See also 'Tourist Information'.
**Scottish Wildlife Trust,** 8 Dublin St., Edinburgh. (031) 556 4199.
**Scottish Youth Hostels Association,** 7 Glebe Crescent, Stirling. (0786) 2821.
**Western Ferries,** 16 Woodside Crescent, Glasgow (041) 332 9766.

## SCOTLAND'S FOOD TABLE

It is hardly surprising that, in a country which measures some 300 miles from its S.W. extremity at Mull of Galloway to its N.E. tip at John o'Groats and about half that distance at its maximum width, there should be considerable variation in the regional specialities available in say, Borders compared with Grampian. And here we are talking purely of the mainland. Add in the island areas (Western Isles, Orkney and Shetland) and you have a selection as diverse as any experienced gourmet could possibly wish for. The following lists of delectable offerings, a mere sprinkling of what is available, is given by way of whetting one's appetite for other 'surprises' which will no doubt be encountered by the visitor during his or her holiday. Some of the dishes, etc. mentioned are to be found in particular parts of the country only and, where this occurs, the region is stated. **ARBROATH SMOKIES.** Salted haddock smoked by traditional method using oak, etc. **BAPS** (Grampian). A fairly large, oval shaped breakfast roll. Delicious with butter. **BLACK BUN.** Normally associated with Festive season. Rich in dried fruit content, particularly currants. Thickish pastry crust surrounds. **BUTTERSCOTCH.** A kind of toffee using brown sugar, ginger and a liberal amount of butter. **CLAPSHOT** (Orkney). Mixture of boiled potatoes/turnips/chives and butter. Onion is sometimes added and the whole is seasoned with salt and pepper. **CLOOTIE DUMPLINGS** (Dumfries and Galloway). A pudding made from self-raising flour, suet, egg, mixed dried fruit, sugar and treacle. The mixture is boiled in a cloth for upwards of 2½ hrs. **COCK-A-LEEKIE.** Soup derived from fowl and leeks. **CRANACHAN** (Highland). A desert using oatmeal, whisky, cream or creamed cheese and sugar to taste. **CROWDIE.** Scotch cream cheese. **CULLEN SKINK** (Grampian). Soup made from smoked haddock, potatoes, onion and milk. **DUNDEE CAKE.** Rich in dried fruit, peel, beaten eggs, flour, almonds, etc. **DUNLOP CHEESE.** Traditionally associated with Dunlop in Ayrshire, now one of the most popular 'hard' cheeses in Scotland. **FORFAR BRIDIES** (Tayside). Minced steak with chopped onion enclosed in pastry case. **GIRDLE SCONES.** Baked on flat iron plate, originally over an open fire. **GROUSE.** This game-bird, richer than chicken, is available on many hotel menus in the period immediately following 12th August — the Glorious Twelfth. **HERRING.** One of the few reasonably-priced fish dishes left in Scotland. Herring fried in oatmeal are delicious, if somewhat bony. **LOCH FYNE KIPPERS** (Strathclyde). Smoked/salted herring. Those from Loch Fyne are particularly sought-after. **OATCAKES.** Oatmeal biscuits made on a hot girdle. Delicious with butter though avoid some of the mass-produced varieties sold in super-markets, etc. **ORKNEY CHEESE** (Orkney). One of the famous cheeses of Scotland, noted for its somewhat salty tang. **PARTAN BREE** (Dumfries and Galloway). Basically a crab soup slightly creamed. **PORRIDGE.** A breakfast time dish of oatmeal boiled in water and served hot usually with a little milk added. The saying goes that no true Scotsman takes sugar on his porridge, though it's commonly done. RUMBLEDETHUMPS (Borders). Mixture of boiled cabbage, potatoes, butter, chives and onions. SALMON. Most famous of all game fish dishes — if you can afford it! Served in a wide variety of ways (e.g. grilled, poached, boiled, kedgeree). Fresh Tay salmon is second to none. SCOTCH BROTH. Extremely popular soup made from mutton pieces, barley and mixed vegetables. SELKIRK BANNOCK (Borders). A lightly fruited loaf. SHORTBREAD. Biscuit-like treat with your cuppa — made with flour, butter and sugar. STOVIES. A stewed dish of sliced potatoes and onion, also sliced. VENISON (Grampian/Highland). Comparatively uncommon on most hotel menus it is, however, found in the regions mentioned. Deer's flesh is not tender and apt to be dry though, if properly cooked and served with natural juices, it can be very fine. HAGGIS. Deliberately kept to the end and placed out of its alphabetical order . . . all because it's probably Scotland's best known 'mystery' dish! Basically haggis is a mixture of sheep's heart, lungs and liver, all finely chopped. Suet, onion and oatmeal are added and the whole is contained in the sheep's stomach-bag (Boiled (often in kitchen foil) the meal is delicious when served with mashed potatoes and turnip. Traditionally associated with Burns' Night (January 25th) for which occasion it is exported worldwide.

## THE SPIRIT OF SCOTLAND

Scotch whisky known the world over — alas sometimes to ill effect! — comes in two quite different types. Although normally of 70 degrees proof, whisky of 100 degrees proof can be bought at any high class licensed grocer throughout the country. Malt whisky, single or double, is made by using the age-old pot-still process from barley hitherto allowed to germinate; grain whisky combines maize and barley (malted and unmalted). Many other contributing factors such as climate, water content, soil and an all-important maturing period of anything from 3-15 years are involved in the vast Scotch whisky-making industry — an industry which is of such financial magnitude that Glasgow alone has about £M1,000 worth stored in its closely guarded warehouses. Little wonder it's known as the 'tinder-box' city! Many of Scotland's famous whisky distilleries encourage visitors to their premises, arrange guided tours and, in some cases fortify you with a free 'dram' as you are about to leave! The following list, by no means exhaustive, indicates certain distilleries throughout Scotland which can be visited — normally Mon./Fri. mornings and afternoons — by the general public. Prior contact

13

with the distillery manager to ascertain precise times is recommended. For convenience, the Region and nearest town/village appearing in the main gazetteer, is bracketed after the distillery's name and location.

AUCHENTOSHAN, Dalmuir (Strathclyde/Glasgow);
BALBLAIR, Edderton. (Highland/Tain);
BALVENIE, Dufftown. (Grampian/Huntly);
BEN NEVIS, Fort William (Highland/Fort William);
BLAIR ATHOLL, Pitlochry. (Tayside/Pitlochry);
BOWMORE, BONAHAVEN, CAOL ILA, BRUICHLADDICH and LAPHROAIG, Isle of Islay. (Strathclyde/Isle of Islay);
CAPERDRONICH, GLEN GRANT — GLENLIVET, Rothes. (Grampian/Elgin);
DEANSTON, Doune. (Central/Dunbalne);
FETTERCAIRN. (Tayside/Brechin);
GIRVAN. (Strathclyde/Girvan);
GLENBURGIE — GLENLIVET, Forres. (Grampian/Forres);
GLENFARCLAS — GLENLIVET, Ballindalloch. (Highland/Grantown-on-Spey);
GLENFIDDICH, Dufftown. (Grampian/Huntly);
GLENKINCHIE, Pencaitland. (Lothian/Haddington);
GLENMORANGIE, Tain. (Highland/Tain);
HIGHLAND PARK, Kirkwall. (Orkney/Orkney Islands);
OBAN. (Strathclyde/Oban);
ST. MAGDALENE, Linlithgow. (Lothian/Linlithgow);
TALISKER, Carbost. (Highland/Isle of Skye);
TOMATIN. (Highland/Inverness);
TULLIBARDINE, Blackford. (Tayside/Auchterarder).

Finally, a phrase well worth knowing—"SLAINTE MHATH" (pron. Slan-ji va) the Gaelic for good health!

# LIFEBOATS

The Royal National Lifeboat Institution has a number of Offshore and Inshore Lifeboats stationed around the coast of Scotland. Some are stations where the lifeboat is in a boathouse, others where the boat lies in the harbour or estuary. Generally speaking, all of these stations may be visited by the general public although there are no set hours for opening as this depends on demand and the ability of the stations to provide attendants. Further information on the RNLI and any of the Stations listed below may be obtained from: The Director, RNLI, West Quay Road, Poole, Dorset. BH15 1HZ.

DUMFRIES and GALLOWAY: **KIRKCUDBRIGHT; PORTPATRICK; KIPPFORD.**
STRATHCLYDE: **GIRVAN; CAMPBELTOWN; ISLAY; TROON; LAMLASH** (Arran); **LARGS; HELENSBURGH;**

TIGHNABRUAICH; OBAN.
HIGHLAND: **MALLAIG; LOCHINVER; THURSO; WICK; INVERGORDON.**
WESTERN ISLES: **BARRA; STORNOWAY.**
ORKNEY: **KIRKWALL; STROMNESS; LONGHOPE.**
SHETLAND: **LERWICK; AITH.**
GRAMPIAN: **BUCKIE; MACDUFF; PETERHEAD; ABERDEEN; STONEHAVEN.**
TAYSIDE: **MONTROSE; ARBROATH; BROUGHTY FERRY.**
FIFE: **ANSTRUTHER; KINGHORN.**
LOTHIAN: **DUNBAR; NORTH BERWICK; QUEENSFERRY.**
BORDERS: **ST. ABBS; EYEMOUTH.**

# RADIO FREQUENCIES

| *VHF* | Radio 1/2 | Radio 3 | Radio Scotland |
|---|---|---|---|
| Kirk o'Shotts | 89.9 | 92.1 | 94.3 |
| Ashkirk | 89.1 | 91.3 | 93.5 |
| Ayr | 88.7 | 90.9 | 93.1 |
| Campbeltown | 88.6 | 90.8 | 93.0 |
| Forfar | 88.3 | 90.5 | 92.7 |
| Lochgilphead | 88.3 | 90.5 | 92.7 |
| Millburn Muir | 88.8 | 91.0 | 93.2 |
| Perth | 89.0 | 91.2 | 93.4 |
| Pitlochry | 89.2 | 91.4 | 93.6 |
| Rosneath | 89.2 | 91.4 | 93.6 |
| Toward | 88.5 | 90.7 | 92.9 |
| Meldrum | 88.7 | 90.9 | 93.1X |
| Bressay | 88.3 | 90.5 | 92.7X— |
| Grantown | 89.8 | 92.0 | 94.2X |
| Kingussie | 89.1 | 91.3 | 93.5X |
| Orkney | 89.3 | 91.5 | 93.7X0 |
| Thrumster | 90.1 | 92.3 | 94.5X |
| Rosemarkie | 89.6 | 91.8 | 94.0∽ |
| Ballachulish | 88.1 | 90.3 | 92.5∽ |
| Fort William | 89.3 | 91.5 | 93.7∽ |
| Kinlochleven | 89.7 | 91.9 | 94.1∽ |
| Melvaig | 89.1 | 91.3 | 93.5∽ |
| Oban | 88.9 | 91.1 | 93.3∽ |
| Penifiler | 89.5 | 91.7 | 93.9∽ |
| Skriaig | 88.5 | 90.7 | 92.9∽ |
| Sandale | 88.1 | 90.3 | 92.5 |

Symbols: XCarries Radio Aberdeen  0Carries Radio Orkney
—Carries Radio Shetland  ∽Carries Radio Highland

*Long and Medium Wave*

| Radio 1 | Frequency k H z | Wavelength metres |
|---|---|---|
| Burghead | 1053 | 285 |
| Westerglen | 1089 | 275 |
| **Radio 2** | | |
| Burghead | 693 | 433 |
| Westerglen | 909 | 330 |
| **Radio 3** | | |
| Westerglen | 1215 | 247 |
| Burghead | 1215 | 247 |
| Redmoss | 1215 | 247 |
| **Radio 4** | | |
| Burghead | 200 | 1500 |
| Westerglen | 200 | 1500 |
| Redmoss | 1449 | 207 |
| **Radio Scotland** | | |
| Burghead | 810 | 371 |
| Westerglen | 810 | 371 |
| Redmoss | 810 | 371 |
| Dumfries | 810 | 371 |

## INDEPENDENT RADIO

| Radio Clyde | 1185 | 261 (and VHF 95.1) |
|---|---|---|
| Radio Forth | 1546 | 194 (and VHF 96.8) |

## MISTAKES

We hope that there aren't any but when you are dealing with literally thousands of facts there may be one or two which have slipped through. The publishers would be most grateful to hear of any that are spotted so that they can be put right in the next edition. So please write to Heritage Publications, Merchants House, Barley Market Street, Tavistock, Devon.

## OPENING TIMES

While every endeavour has been made to ensure accuracy, some opening days and times are bound to be changed after we went to press.

# DOGS

Not normally admitted to houses, mansions, National Trust for Scotland properties, museums or art galleries unless otherwise stated.

# REGIONALISATION

Following the reform of Local Government in Scotland, the undernoted new Regions were created, and became administratively effective, in 1975. The counties now largely embraced by these 12 Regions are shown in brackets although, for the purpose of this guide, these do not appear against the main entries in the gazetteer.

DUMFRIES and GALLOWAY (Dumfries, Kirkcudbright, Wigtown).
BORDERS (Berwick, Roxburgh, Selkirk, Peebles).
LOTHIAN (East Lothian, Midlothian, West Lothian).
STRATHCLYDE (Lanark, Renfrew, Dumbarton, Ayr, Bute, Argyll).
CENTRAL (Stirling, Clackmannan).
FIFE (Fife).
TAYSIDE (Angus, Perth, Kinross).
HIGHLAND (Inverness, Nairn, Ross and Cromarty, Caithness, Sutherland).
GRAMPIAN (Aberdeen, Kincardine, Moray, Banff).
WESTERN ISLES (Inverness — part, Ross and Cromarty — part).
ORKNEY (Orkney).
SHETLAND (Zetland).

# SCOTLAND'S GARDENS SCHEME

Apart from the gardens mentioned under some of the entries appearing in the gazetteer section of this guide, there are a great many more which are open to visitors at a time of year they are expected to be looking at their best. Full details of these, their times of opening, etc., can be obtained by writing to: Scotland's Gardens Scheme, 26 Castle Terrace, Edinburgh, EH1 2EL.

# SYMBOLS/ABBREVIATIONS

In addition to the umbrella symbol for places which provide shelter on a wet day, five others are used through the book to help the reader identify the place he is seeking quickly. These, together with certain abbreviations also used, are:

⟋ a walking stick pin-points places around which, from which or to which walks may be enjoyed;

🏃 the sign for children picks out those places which provide entertainment or information particularly for children;

⚑ the region covered has a number of points from which good views can be enjoyed and these are identified with this symbol;

🐾 for some perhaps the most important symbol of all — the symbol for quiet places. There aren't many left where genuine peace can be obtained and most entail walking away from the recognised tourist focal point.

ℓ places where tourist information is available.

W places open in the winter; (churches are not marked as they are normally open all year)

**N.T.S.** stands for National Trust for Scotland;

**D.E.** for Department of the Environment;

**Dumf. & Gall.** for Dumfries and Galloway.

Throughout Scotland, Tourist Information Centres provide visitors with all manner of informative data and assistance to help you discover and enjoy the region. The staff at these centres deal with several hundred enquiries each week and are well qualified to answer most of your queries about their particular part of the country. Appearing below are offices (open all year) which are geared to provide information on the area in which they are located and, in some cases, on Scotland as a whole. The list is arranged alphabetically and therefore bears no relation to the geography of the country.

BORDERS: Borders Regional Council (Tourism), Newton St. Boswells (083 52) 3301;

CENTRAL: Central Regional Council (Tourism) Viewforth, Stirling (0786) 3111;

DUMFRIES and GALLOWAY: Tourist Association, Newton Stewart (0671) 2549;

FIFE: Tourist Authority, North St., Glenrothes (0592) 754411;

GRAMPIAN: Grampian Regional Council (Tourism), Woodhill House, Ashgrove Rd., West, Aberdeen (0224) 23401;

HIGHLAND: Highlands and Islands Tourism Council, 54 High St., Grantown-on-Spey (0479) 2773;

LOTHIAN: Lothian Regional Council (Tourism), 40 Torphichen St., Edinburgh (031) 229 9292;

ORKNEY: Tourist Association, Kirkwall (0856) 2856;

SHETLAND: Tourist Organisation, Alexandra Wharf, Lerwick (0595) 3434;

STRATHCLYDE: Strathclyde Regional Council (Tourism), McIver House, 51 Cadogan St., Glasgow.

TAYSIDE: Tayside Regional Council (Tourism), 26 Crichton St., Dundee (0382) 23281;

WESTERN ISLES: Tourist Association, South Beach Quay, Stornoway (0851) 3088.

Other useful addresses:

ABERDEEN (City); Aberdeen District Council, St. Nicholas House, Broad St., Aberdeen (0224) 23456;

DUNDEE: 16 City Square, Dundee (0382) 27723;

EDINBURGH: 5 Waverley Bridge, Edinburgh (031) 226 6591;

GLASGOW: George Square, Glasgow (041) 221 7371/2.

# "SEE ALSO" REFERENCES

Users of this guide should note that at the end of most main headings within the gazetteer a SEE ALSO reference has been added. In all cases this implies that the places then mentioned are worth visiting while in the actual town or village being described. It does not mean that a text of these subsidiary places will necessarily be found elsewhere in the gazetteer.

# THE GAZETTEER

The use of the gazetteer has been made as simple as possible. Beside the town on the top line is the population to the nearest 500 and the early closing days — E.C. Where a place to visit is featured the opening times are given in italics. Those owned by the National Trust for Scotland are identified as **N.T.S.** Those places under the care of the Department of the Environment are identified by **D.E.** While every care has been taken to be accurate with the opening times, circumstances can and do change and so might the opening times. Normally the word "summer" before the opening times indicates that the place will be open from Easter to the end of September or mid-October. No prices of admission are included as it is virtually impossible to be accurate about them in these inflationary times. The abbreviation m. is used for miles and the first letter for points of the compass. Centuries are abbreviated to c. The use of a c. in front of a date indicates an approximation. In addition the following symbols appear beside the text:

🐘 places which provide shelter on a wet day;

╱ places from which or upon which walks can be enjoyed;

🏃 places which in particular provide entertainment for children;

⋇ a viewpoint;

🦌 quiet places where you can normally get away from it all;

𝒾 places where tourist information is available.

W places open in the winter — churches which are open all year are not marked.

**ABERDEEN,** Grampian    179,500    E.C. Wed.
62 m. E. of Braemar by A93; 106 m. S.E. of Inverness by A96; 83 m. N.E. of Perth by A94/A92.

𝒾 St. Nicholas House, Broad St. (0224) 23456.

𝒾 Caravan, Stonehaven Rd. (0224) 873030.

**Weather:** (0224) 722331.

Largest holiday resort in Scotland with good 2 m. sand beach and varied entertainment. Sparkling granite buildings predominate, hence named 'The Granite City'. Frequent winner of Britain in Bloom contest. Famous University and fishmarket. North Sea Oil 'boom' town. Touring centre for Royal Deeside and Don valley.

🐘 **Art Gallery and Museum.** Blackfriars St. *10-5 weekdays (ex.*
W *Thurs. 10-8) 2-5 Sun.* Interesting collection of British paintings and sculptures, mainly 20th c.

**⋔ James Dun's House.** Schoolhill. *10-5 weekdays.* Museum for children.

**Brig o' Balgownie.** ¾ m. N. of High St. Oldest medieval bridge in Scotland. 62 ft. wide Gothic arch.

**St. Machar's Cathedral.** Chanonry, off St. Machar Dr. Founded 1157 on site of 6th c. Celtic church. Main building dates from mid-15th c. West front (towers) outstanding.

**King's College.** High St. *9-5 weekdays.* Founded 1495. 17th c. 'crown' tower and interesting woodwork in chapel.

**Marischal College.** Broad St. With King's (above) forms w Aberdeen University. Impressive building founded 1593, one of finest granite structures in world. *Museum 9-5 Mon. to Fri. (ex. Thurs.) 9-5 and 6-9.30 Thurs.; 9-12 and 2.30-5.30 Sat.; 2.30-5.30 Sun.* Contains many Egyptian and Chinese antiquities.

**Provost Ross's House. (N.T.S.)** Shiprow. *2.30-4.30 Mon.-*
w *Fri.* Built 1593. Depicts early Scottish domestic architecture. One of Aberdeen's oldest houses. Restored in 1954.

**Provost Skene's House.** Broad St. *10-5 weekdays.* Built about
w 1545. Contains period furniture, interesting painted ceilings and relics of Aberdeen's evolution. Duke of Cumberland stayed here prior to defeat of Prince Charles Edward at Culloden (1745).

**⋔ Fish Market.** Near Albert Basin. Rise early and be there by 7.30. *(Mon.-Fri.)* Reward . . . see the trawlers unload their catches at Scotland's largest fishing port and the auctions that follow.

**Aberdeen Highland Games.** *Annually (June).*

**International Festival of Youth Orchestras** *(August).*
See also HAZLEHEAD PARK (Maze, etc.), ABERDEEN AIRPORT (Dyce)/HELIPORT, BRIDGE OF DEE.

**ABERFELDY,** Tayside    1,500    E.C. Wed.
31 m. N.W. of Perth by A9/A827; 14 m. S.W. of Pitlochry by A827/A9.

*ℓ* The Square (088 72) 276.

Attractive town set in delightful surroundings near R. Tay. Birks (meaning silver birch) of Aberfeldy close by.

**Wade's Bridge.** Spans R. Tay. Regarded as finest built (1733) by General Wade.

**Castle Menzies.** 1 m. W. by B846. *Apr. to Oct. 10-12.30, 2-4.30 Sat., 2-4.30 Sun.* Good example of 16th c. Scottish mansion. Carved dormers added in 1577.

21

**St. Mary's Church.** 2 m. N.E. by A827. Dates from 16th c. Fine painted ceiling.

**Yew Tree.** Fortingall. 9 m. W. by B846 thence Fortingall road. Tree said to be over 3,000 yrs. old, a probable British record.

**Highland Games.** *Annually in Aug.*

See also KENMORE, GRANDTULLY, GLEN LYON.

**ABERFOYLE,** Central    1,000    E.C. Wed.
20 m. W. of Stirling by A84/A873; 27 m. N. of Glasgow by A81.

*i* Main St. (087 72) 352.

Large village on R. Forth in heart of Rob Roy country. One of several 'gateways' to Trossachs. Flanked by Achray Forest and Queen Elizabeth Forest Park. Much frequented as a stopping-off point for 'mystery' coach tours from Glasgow, etc. **Duke's Pass** (A821) winds N. to offer fine views over Loch Venachar and so to Trossachs (6 miles). Surrounding area provides setting for Sir Walter Scott's novels 'Rob Roy' and 'Lady of the Lake'.

**David Marshall Lodge.** Off A821 just N. of village. Owned by Forestry Commission. Collection of stuffed wildlife. Commands excellent panoramic views to S. Fine woodland walks.

**Trossachs,** meaning 'bristly country', extends W. from Loch Achray to E. end of Loch Katrine. Possibly most visited rural area in Scotland on account of fine scenery and easy access from Glasgow and Edinburgh. Given good weather a steamer cruise on L. Katrine by 'Sir Walter Scott', built 1900 and assembled on lochside, is a memorable experience.

**Inchmahome Priory. D.E.** 3 m. E. off A873. *Apr. to Sept.* W *9.30-7; Oct. to Mar. 9.30-4.* Situated on small island on Lake of Menteith, Scotland's only lake . . . ferry from Port of Menteith. Founded c. 1238. David II married here. Home too of Mary, Queen of Scots for one year.

See also GARTMORE, KINLOCHARD, STRONACH-LACHAR, INVERSNAID.

**ABOYNE,** Grampian    1,000    E.C. Thurs.
31 m. W. of Aberdeen by A93; 28 m. E. of Braemar by A93.
Well known for its Highland Games (Sept.) Good centre for walking. Glen Tanar to S. is particularly attractive.

**Tomnaverie Stone Circle. D.E.** 4 m. N.W. by B9094. Stone circle remains dating from 1800-1600 B.C.

See also KINCARDINE O'NEIL, LUMPHANAN, TARLAND.


**ALFORD,** Grampian     1,000     E.C. Wed.
26 m. W. of Aberdeen by A944; 22 m. S. of Huntly by A97/A944.

Pleasant little town on R. Don. Good centre for exploring much-loved Donside.

🦔 **Craigievar Castle. N.T.S.** 7 m. S. off A980. *May to Sept. 2-7 Wed. Thurs. Sun.; first fortnight Oct. 2-6. Also Jul. and Aug. 2-7 Sat.* Completed 1626 and remained unaltered ever since. Noteworthy is great tower, turreted roof and fine hall with intricately worked plaster ceiling.

**Kildrummy Castle and Gardens. D.E.** 10 m. W off A97. *Castle open all reasonable times. Gardens: Apr. to Oct. 9-5.* Founded early 13th c. One of most historic castles in Grampian region. Edward I was responsible for murder of Robert the Bruce's brother. Seat of Earls of Mar. Plans were here drawn up for 1715 rebellion. Chapel gable (interior building) is probably most noteworthy part of remains. **Gardens:** Japanese water-garden, shrubs, trees, etc., of considerable interest.

See also MONYMUSK, GLENBUCHAT.

**ANNAN,** Dumf. & Gall.  6,000  E.C. Wed.
19 m. N.W. of Carlisle by A75/A74/A7; 16 m. S.E. of Dumfries by A75.

Solidly built town near mouth of R..Annan. Atomic Energy Establishment at Chapelcross absorbs much of the local workforce. Academy holds distinction of having had Thomas Carlyle on teaching staff.

**Carlyle's Birthplace. N.T.S.** Ecclefechan. 7 m. N. by B722. *Mar. to Oct. 10-6 daily ex. Sun.* Thomas Carlyle born here 1795. Interesting letters, etc. on view.

**Ruthwell Cross. D.E.** Ruthwell Church 6 m. W. by B725. Dates from 8th c. Anglican sculpture at its finest. This 18 ft. high cross is reminder of dark age Europe.
Note the carved poem, sometimes known as "Dream of the Cross". Verse, in first person, contains several of the earliest phrases written in English.

**Duncan Museum.** Named after Rev. Henry Duncan who set up the country's first savings bank in 1810.

**ARBROATH,** Tayside  *23,000*  *E.C. Wed.*
18 m. N.E. of Dundee by A92; 15 m S.E. of Forfar by A933/A932.

*ℓ* 105 High St. (0241) 2609/6680

Fishing port and holiday resort of some significance. Boasts one of country's largest open-air heated swimming-pools. Good sand beaches. Much fine cliff scenery to N. of town. Created a royal burgh in 1599.

w **Abbey Church. D.E.** *Apr. to Sept. 9.30-7 weekdays, 2-7 Sun; Oct. to Mar. 9.30-4 weekdays, 2-4 Sun.* Declaration of Arbroath (1320) here signed giving Scotland independence after Bruce's victory at Bannockburn. Well preserved fine red sandstone ruin; especially cloisters. Abbot's House is now museum with interesting works of Scottish medieval art. See also **St. Vigean's Museum** (not Sun.) N.W. outskirts of town,

24

for rare collection of sculptured stones (Pictish and Celtic Early Christian).

🐘 **Kellie Castle.** 3 m. W. by B9127. Part at least dates from 1170. Tower late 15th c. Presently lived in, the castle has fine gallery where contemporary artists and craftsmen exhibit their works. *April-Dec., 10.30-5.30 ex. Tues.*

🐘 **Signal Tower Museum.** *All year 9.30-1; 2-5 daily (Ex. Sun.).*
W Catch up on the local history of the town and the work of its people over the years.

**Arbroath Agricultural Show.** *July.*

See also AUCHMITHIE

**ARRAN**, Strathclyde   3,500   E.C. Wed.
Island in Firth of Clyde with ferry connections from mainland. Ardrossan — Brodick (1 hr.). Claonaig (Kintyre) — Lochranza (30 mins.).

*ℓ* The Pier (0770) 2140.

Measures approx. 20 m. by 10 m. Has thriving tourist industry due partly to easy access from Glasgow. Brodick is principle township. Whiting Bay, Lamlash, Blackwaterfoot and Lochranza also popular. 'Round the island' coach tour is laziest way of seeing much in short time!

🐘 **Brodick Castle. N.T.S.** *Easter to Sept. 1-5 weekdays; 2-5 Sun.*
W *Castle Gardens open all year 10-5.* Seat of Dukes of Hamilton. Minor part dates from 14th c. Main structure from 1845. Fine collection of silver, china and other treasures including paintings. The Gardens, especially the rhododendrons, are well worth seeing.

⚹ **Goat Fell** (2866 ft.) **N.T.S.** Highest mountain on island. Rewarding view from top. You may see a golden eagle on way up.

**Machrie Moor Standing Stones. D.E.** 8 m. W. by 'String Road'. 15 ft. high stones form Bronze Age circle.

**Sea Angling Festival.** *May.*

**Highland Games** (Brodick) *August.*

See also KILMORY, LAGG, DIPPIN.

**ARROCHAR**, Strathclyde   543
17 m. N. of Helensburgh by A.814; 1½ m. W. of Tarbet (Loch Lomon) by A.83.

*ℓ* (Tarbet-Stuckgowan 2 m.) (030 12) 251.

Attractive little village set at head of 16 m. long Loch Long, popular with anglers. Nearby are some of Argyll's finest peaks notably Ben Arthur otherwise known as the "Cobbler". Excellent rock climbing on this 2,891 ft. mountain and on Beinn Narnain (3,066 ft) to N.E.

**Rest and be Thankful.** 6 m. W. by A.83. (806 ft.) Name originally given to stone seat in Glen Croe. Apt and necessary with fierce gradients in by-gone days. Present road skirts pleasant Croe Water with views to Argyll Forest Park, Britain's oldest (1935). Original road still used for competitive car hill climbs.

See also LOCHGOILHEAD.

**AUCHTERARDER,** Tayside.     3,000     E.C. Wed.
14 m. S.W. of Perth by A9; 20 m. N.E. of Stirling by A9.

Noted for extremely long main street (about 1½ mls.). Town burned down (1715) by Earl of Mar after battle of Sheriffmuir. Nearby is sumptuous Gleneagles Hotel, Scotland's only ***** hotel.

**Strathallan Aircraft Collection.** 3 m. N. off B.8062. Rapidly expanding museum includes a Lancaster, Mosquito and Hurricane and many other famous aircraft dating back to 1930. Engines, photographs and Comet airliner museum. *Special air display, July 12, 13. Daily, 10-5 (dusk in winter). Tel: Auchterarder 2545 for further details.*

**Tullibardine Chapel.** 3 m. N.W. off A823. *Apr. to Sept. 9.30-7 weekdays, 2-7 Sun.; Oct. to Mar. 9.30-4 weekdays, 2-4 Sun.* Founded 1446. Collegiate church remains unaltered and is almost unique in Scotland. Of special interest is open roof and heraldic detail.

**Ardoch Roman Camp.** 5 m. W. by unclass road, near A822. Remains of Roman camps, early 2 c. One of largest in Britain.

See also DUNNING, GLEN DEVON.

**AVIEMORE,** Highland.   1,800   E.C. Wed.
29 m. S. of Inverness by A.9; 13 m. W. of Grantown on Spey by A.95.

**Aviemore Centre.** Open all-year with all-weather attractions for the family and the sportsman including 25m indoor heated leisure pool, Britain's biggest all-year ice rink, squash, dry ski slopes with tow, Kart raceway, crazy golf, cinema, live entertainments, disco, saunas, solarium, restaurants and tuition and equipment hire for skiing, windsurfing, sailing, canoeing and fishing. Highland Craft Village square of traditional craftsmen's shops, and two other shopping centres.

**Santa Claus Land** (Part of Aviemore Centre). Santa Claus in

HURRICANE
LANCASTER ▪ HARVARD
TIGER MOTH ▪ MAGISTER
MOSQUITO ▪ SHACKLETON
COMET ▪ LEOPARD MOTH
MOTH MINOR ▪ SWALLOW
DESFORD ▪ PROVOST
SCION ▪ DRAGON
LYSANDER ▪ ANSON
BOLINGBROKE ▪ BATTLE

ONLY PART OF
THE LARGEST PRIVATE
AIRCRAFT COLLECTION
IN SCOTLAND

STRATHALLAN
AIRCRAFT
COLLECTION

# aviemore CENTRE

YOUR HOLIDAY HIGHLIGHT

So much to do. Santa Claus Land, skating-curling-ice hockey rink, 25m indoor heated leisure pool with saunas, solarium, bike hire, and squash courts. Dry ski slopes, one with tow. Browse in three shopping centres including the renowned Highland Craft Village.

Night life for all ages — disco, dancing, live enter-tainments and new-release films in the Speyside Theatre. Wine and dine — choose from the Das Stubel Austrian-style grill, Pinewood restaurant and three snack bars. Visit the Senn Hutte, Deerstalker and Ice Rink bars.

Explore the history of the beautiful Spey Valley. An-cient monuments, hill-walks, wildlife galore — and every facility for windsurfing, canoeing, sailing, fishing — and the family picnic.

Easy by train, easy by car. The Aviemore Centre is one minute's walk from the station. Tremendous value with weekend returns, Great Rail Club, Family and Senior Citizen's Railcards. The A9 improvements mean an easy journey to our doorstep. Park your car and relax in the Aviemore Centre.

Leaflets and Enquiries:
General Manager (Box 248), Aviemore Centre, Aviemore, Inverness-shire. Tel: 0479  810624.

log cabin toyshop. Sleigh, veteran car and Alice in Santa Land rides. Pony trek through Wild West OK Corrall. Pogo stick park, stilts, pets farms, ruined castle. Feel the ice-covered North Pole!

**Scotland's Clan Tartan Centre** (Part of the Aviemore Centre). Display of Highland tartans and woollen goods. Mini-theatre with audio-visual about the tartan. Archive computer with 10,000 family histories which issues permanent certificates showing history, development, war cry, tartan of each clan.

**Landmark Visitor Centre.** Carrbridge. 7 m. N. by A9. Depicts history of Strath Spey from last Ice Age to present day. Audio-visual presentation in small theatre. Well-stocked craft shop. Pleasant forest walks.

**Strathspey Railway Association.** 7 m. N.E. off A95 at Boat of Garten. Enquire locally re. viewing. Formerly station on Highland Railway (closed 1965) now being redeveloped as museum and working line to Aviemore. Rolling stock and engines of bygone days.

**Loch Garten Nature Reserve.** 8 m. N.E. off B970. *Mid Apr. to mid Aug. daily.* Breeding ospreys have returned here yearly since 1959. Viewpoint from hide through binoculars.

**Loch-an-Eilean Visitor Centre.** 3 m. S. by B970. Nature trail along shore of lovely loch. Exhibition depicts history of Scots pine through the ages.

**Highland Wildlife Park.** 8 m. S.W. off A9. *Apr. to Sept. 10-6.* Like a safari park though with emphasis on Highland animals and birds. Fine natural setting. Red deer, eagles, wildcat can be seen.

See also SLUGGAN BRIDGE.

**AYR,** Strathclyde     48,000     E.C. Wed.
33 m. S.W. of Glasgow by A77; 22 m. N.E. of Girvan by A77.
30 Miller Rd. (0292) 68077.

Thriving holiday resort on Firth of Clyde. Much frequented by work-worn residents of Glasgow and environs. Focal point of Burns country. Good shops and ample entertainment for adults and children. Boasts one of best beaches in S.W. Scotland. Racecourse holds regular meetings. Ice rink.

**Tam o'Shanter Inn.** High St. *Apr. to Sept. 9.30-5.30 week-days; Oct. to Mar. 12-4.* Now a museum with interesting relics. Thought to be starting point of ride described in famous poem.

**Auld Brig.** Wallace St./High St. Spans R. Ayr. Dates from 13th c. Features in Burns' 'Two Brigs.'

**Burns Cottage.** Alloway. 2 m. S. by B7024. *Mar. to Oct. 9-7* w *weekdays; May, Sept. Oct. 2-7 Sun; Jun. Jul. and Aug. 10-7 Sun; Nov. to Apr. 10-4 weekdays.* Birthplace of Scotland's greatest poet (1759-1796). Contains interesting items though for larger collection see adjoining museum. Pleasant garden. Attracts more than 100,000 visitors annually.

**Alloway Kirk.** Alloway (see above). The poet's character Tam o'Shanter here watched witches' orgy. Here too Burns' father is buried.

**Burns Monument.** Alloway. Dates from 1820. Rightly described as 'startling'. See garden with figures of Burns characters.

**Brig o'Doon.** Alloway. Single arch spans R. Doon. About 13th c. Features greatly in Burns' 'Tam o'Shanter'.

**Land o'Burns Visitor Centre.** Alloway. *Easter and Oct. 10*✷*6* w *daily; Summer 10-9; Winter 10-4.* Interesting exhibition centre with audio-visual theatre in 'Landmark' style. Souvenir shop.

**Bachelors' Club.** Tarbolton. **N.T.S.** 8 m. N.E. by B744 off A758. Enquiries to 28 Croft St. Tarbolton. Literary and debating society founded by Burns and friends (1780). Here poet became freemason.

**Burns Monument and Museum.** Kilmarnock. 13 m. N.E. by w A77. *Apr. to Sept. 12.30-8.30 Mon. and Wed./Sat. Oct. to Apr. 10-5 Mon. and Wed./Sat.* Houses valuable collection of Burns manuscripts and books including the priceless first (Kilmarnock) edition of his poems.

**Auchinleck Church and Boswell Mausoleum.** 14 m. E. by A70/A76. Enquiries re. guided tour tel. (0290) 20757. Parish Church, once Celtic cell, dates from 12th c. James Boswell, Dr. Johnson's famous biographer, buried in mausoleum.

**Ayr Flower Show** (Dam Park). *August.*

See also MAUCHLINE, PRESTWICK (Airport), TROON.

**BALLATER,** Grampian  1,000  E.C. Thur.
16 m. E. of Braemar by A.93; 42 m. W. of Aberdeen by A.93
*i* Station Square (033 82) 306.

Excellent touring centre for Deeside, particularly popular in late summer when Royal Family normally take vacation in nearby Balmoral Castle. Good accommodation in town and ✷ grand scenery, notably 3,786 ft. Lochnagar, much-climbed peak in Cairngorm range.

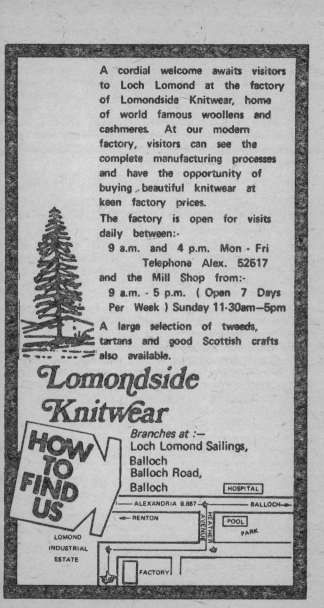

**Balmoral Castle.** 8 m. W. by A.93. Property of Her Majesty the Queen. Grounds only open. *May-July, daily ex. Sun., 10-5.*

**Crathie Church.** 7 m. W. by A.93. Neat little granite building (1895). Used as place of worship by Royal Family during visits to Balmoral. Royal gifts may be seen. *All reasonable times.*

**Birkhall.** 1 m. S. by minor (Glen Muick) road. Formerly property of Edward VII. 18th c. house now used periodically by Queen Mother. *No admission.*

**Ballater Highland Gathering.** *August.*

See also LOCH MUICK, BRIDGE OF TULLICH.

**BALLOCH,** Strathclyde   1,500   E.C. Wed.
18 m. N.W. of Glasgow and 8 m. S. of Luss by A.82.

Information centre (0389) 53533.

Highly popular little town at S. end of L. Lomond. Lies astride fast-flowing R. Leven, here packed with houseboats and other small craft. Terminus of Glasgow-Balloch "Blue Train" electric line. Starting point for steamer cruises on L. Lomond by paddle-steamer, "Maid of the Loch".

**Lomondside Knitwear.** Lomond Ind. Est. — outskirts. Home of world famous woollens and cashmeres. See complete manufacturing process in factory. *Mon.-Fri., 9-4. Mill shop: daily 9-5, Sun. 11.30-5.*

**Cameron Loch Lomond.** 1 m. N. by old Luss road. Much-visited bear park with famous Loch Lomond bears. Also bison, yak, rare sheep, deer and zoo garden. Historic house with interesting whisky bottle collection. Children's play area and restaurant with tranquil waters of Loch Lomond skirting the park. *Apr.-mid.-Oct., 7.30-6 daily.* **See ad at back.**

**Balloch Park.** Pleasant place to walk and enjoy views of lovely Loch Lomond. Magnificent trees and well-kept flower garden.

**BANCHORY,** Grampian   1,000   E.C. Thurs.
18 m. W. of Aberdeen by A93; 40 m. E. of Braemar by A93.

Dee St. Car Park (033 02) 2000.

Pleasantly situated on R. Dee. Centre for lavender growing and distilling (see factory). Good nature trails nearby.

**Wee Museum.** *Apr. to Sept. 10-5 (Mon.).* Exhibits akin to Banchory and environs.

**Bridge of Feugh** (below town to S.) Favourite spot to watch the salmon leaping . . . given the right conditions.

🐦 **Crathes Castle and Gardens. N.T.S.** 4 m. E. off A93. *Castle: Apr. and Oct. 11-1, 2-6 (Wed.) 2-6 (Sat./Sun.) May to Sept. 11-6 (Mon./Fri.) 2-6 (Sat./Sun.). Gardens open from 9.30 daily.* L-plan tower-house with several decorative turrets, etc. Completed 1594. Interior has fine painted ceilings. Oak-panelled ceiling in Long Gallery unique in Scotland. Visitor Centre. Gardens have excellent collection of trees and shrubs. Yew hedges date from 1702.

🐦 **Drum Castle. N.T.S.** 9 m. E. off A93. *Mid Jul. to Sept. 11-5 weekdays; 2-6 Sun. Oct. 11-1, 2-6 Wed. 2-6 Sat. Sun.* Acquired by National Trust for Scotland in 1975. Granite built tower of 1272. Conferred by Robert the Bruce (1324) on William de Irvin, his standard bearer. Mansion (1619) has fine furniture and silver.

See also ECHT, CAIRN O' MOUNT/B974 (view).

**BANFF,** Grampian     4,000     E.C. Wed.
47 m. N.W. of Aberdeen by A947; 21 m. N.E. of Huntly by A97.

*i* Collie Lodge (026 12) 2419.

Lively fishing port on R. Deveron. Bridge connects with Macduff.

🐦 **Duff House. D.E.** *Apr. to Sept. 9.30-7 weekdays, 2-7 Sun.* Former seat of Earl of Fife. Adams mansion is one of the finest examples of Georgian architecture in Scotland. Said to be copy of Rome's Villa Borghese.

🐦 **Delgatie Castle.** 12 m. S.E. off A947. Enquiries re. admission (Tel. (088 82) 3479. Dates from 13th c. Tower home of Hays for c. 700 yrs. Pictures, arms and fine painted ceilings. See room used by Mary, Queen of Scots in 1562.

**Portsoy.** 8 m. W. by B9139. Well known for its serpentine marble. Used in Palace of Versailles. Souvenirs available locally.

See also CULLEN, TURRIFF, PENNAN.

**BARRA,** Western Isles     1,000
Car ferry from Oban (5½ hrs.)

*i* Castlebay (087 14) 336.

Measures 8 m. by 4 m. Barren in parts with fine sand beaches on W. Setting of film 'Whisky Galore'. 1,000 different wild flowers earn it the name 'Garden of Hebrides'. Castlebay is steamer port and island 'capital'.

🐦 **Kisimul Castle.** Reached by hired boat from Castlebay. *May/Sept. Wed. and Sat. (afternoon).* Dates from c. 1060.

33

Home of the Macneils of Barra from 1314. Completely
restored 1970.

Cockle Strand. Sandy bay at N. end of island. Civil airport
unique in Britain as plane timings are subject to state of tide!
Near here is buried the Scots author Sir Compton Mackenzie.

See also VATERSAY (ferry).


**BLAIRGOWRIE,** Tayside    5,500    E.C. Thurs.
19 m. N.W. of Dundee by A923; 16 m. N. of Perth by A93.

*i* Wellmeadow (0250) 2960.

Raspberry farms much in evidence around this pleasant town
on R. Ericht. Half of Scotland's annual crop produced hereabouts. Good holiday centre for exploring the Howe of
Strathmore and Strath Ardle.

**Beech Hedge, Meikleour.** 5 m. S. by A93. Planted in 1746 this
famous hedge is presently 85 ft. high and extends to almost
600 yards. Thought to be highest of its kind in world.

Meigle Museum. D.E. 8 m. E. by A926/A927. *Apr. to Sept.*
W *9.30-7 weekdays; Oct. to Mar. 9.30-4 weekdays.* Outstanding
collection of almost 30 sculptured stones from 7th-10th c.
Exhibits considered to be finest examples of Dark Age
sculptures in Western Europe.

**Blairgowrie Highland Games.** *July.*

See also COUPAR ANGUS, ALYTH, KIRKMICHAEL.


**BRAEMAR,** Grampian    E.C. Thurs. (out of season).
62 m. W. of Aberdeen by A93; 34 m. N. of Blairgowrie by
A93.

*i* Fife Arms Mews. (033 83) 600.

Picturesquely set near upper reaches of R. Dee. Venue for
Scotland's "V.I.P." Highland Games — the Royal Highland
Gathering *(Sept.).* Good walking centre and base from which
to climb Ben Macdhui (4296 ft.), the country's second highest
mountain.

Braemar Castle. *May to Oct. 10 - 6. daily.* Built by Earl of
Mar (1628). English soldiers garrisoned here after 1715 and
1745 Jacobite risings. Interesting round central tower, vaulted
halls and pit prison. Son et Lumière during Aug. and Sept.

**The Mound.** Plaque in local hotel marks spot where Earl of
Mar raised standard at 1715 rising.

**Balmoral Castle.** 8 m. E. by A93. Impressive white granite
structure begun in 1853. Considered to be H.M. The Queen's

best loved residence while holidaying in Britain. Admission to castle grounds only (not when Royal Family in residence).

🐾 **Crathie Church.** A93 slightly E. of Balmoral Castle. *All reasonable times.* Neat little granite building built 1895. Used as place of worship by Royal Family during visits to Castle. Contains royal gifts.

🎿 **Glenshee Chairlift.** 10 m. S. off A93. 9-4.30. Like Aviemore and Glencoe — another well organised Scottish ski centre. Dry-ski run (summer). Chairlift, if you have head for heights, takes you 1,000 ft. up. Cairnwell Pass rising to 2199 ft. is Britain's highest main road (A93) pass.

**Ballater and Lonach Highland Gatherings.** *August.*

See also LINN OF DEE, BALLATER, GLEN MUICK.

**BRECHIN,** Tayside     6,500     E.C. Wed.
9 m. W. of Montrose by A935; 13 m. N.E. of Forfar by A94.

Famous above all for Cathedral with Round Tower. Excellent centre for much-loved Angus Glens — notably Clova, Prosen and Esk.

**Cathedral and Round Tower.** Viewed from churchyard. Cathedral founded 1150 by David I. Choir is fine example of lancet work. See also W. window and portal. Interesting 10th-13th c. tombstones. Round tower (87 ft.) erected between 990 and 1012. This, and round tower at Abernethy, (see Perth) are only two remaining round towers on Scottish mainland.

**The Caterthuns. D.E.** *All times.* 5 m. N.W. by unclass. road. Remains of Iron Age hill forts.

w **Edzell Castle. D.E.** 6 m. N. off B996. *Apr. to Sept. 9.30-7 weekdays, 2-7 Sun; Oct. to Mar. 9.30-4 weekdays, 2-4 Sun.* Walled garden, the 'Pleasance' (built 1604) is outstanding feature. Has heraldic and symbolic sculptures unique in Scotland. Formal garden is worthy of attention. Castle dates from 16th c. Now a ruin.

🐾 **Glenesk Folk Museum** (Tarfside hamlet). 16 m. N.W. by unclass. road. *Easter weekend and Suns. to end May. June to Sept. 2-6 daily.* Depicts life in typical Angus glen from early 19th c. to present day.

See also FETTERCAIRN, ABERLEMNO.

**CALLANDER,** Central     2,000     E.C. Wed.
53 m. N.W. of Edinburgh by M9/A84; 16 m. N.W. of Stirling by A84.

ℓ Leny Rd. (0877) 30342.

Gateway to Highlands in truest sense. Solidly built town on

R. Teith. Packed with touring coaches during season. Tweed and souvenir shops a-plenty and even a mini-fun fair. Be there on a Sat. around 8 p.m. and hear the local pipe band (off Main St.).

**Bracklinn Falls.** N. of town by unclass. road via golf course. A noted beauty spot with fine views. On way you pass Arden House, setting for T.V. series 'Dr. Finlay's Casebook'.

**Invertrossachs Nature Reserve.** 5 m. W. on S. shore L. Venachar. Established 1976. Observation hides. Wild animals. Over 90 species of birds. Nature trails. Children's collection.

**Leny Falls.** 3 m. W. by A84. Impressive falls on fast-flowing river. Here Highlanders once hid from English Redcoats.

**Strathyre.** 8 m. N.W. by A84. Famed in song 'Bonnie Strathyre'. Considered by many to be Scotland's prettiest village. Memorial to Dugald Buchanan, Gaelic poet.

**Rob Roy's Grave.** Balquhidder. 14 m. N.W. by A84 and unclass. road. Little churchyard with tombstones to Rob Roy (died 1734) and his family. Braes of Balquhidder which flank N. side of nearby L. Voil are outstandingly beautiful.

See also BRIG O' TURK, DOUNE.

**CAMPBELTOWN;** Strathclyde    6,000    E.C. Wed.
38 m. S. of Tarbert (Loch Fyne) by A83; 89 m. S. of Oban by A816/A83.
*i* Mid Argyll, Kintyre and Islay Tourist Organisation (0586) 2056.

Fishing port and holiday resort near S. tip of Kintyre. Ex-Beatle Paul McCartney's "Mull of Kintyre" has surprisingly done much for local tourist industry here. 5 m. W. by B843 is Machrihanish noted for its golf course and splendid sand beach.

**Campbeltown Cross,** Main St. 15th c. cross with intricate ornamentation and inscription in Lombardic letters.

**Davaar Island.** (Entrance to Campbeltown Loch). A true island only at high tide. Normally reached via the Dhorlin shingle bank east of town. See painting of Crucifixion in island cave. Dates from 1887. Said to have been inspired by dream.

**Keil.** 10 m. S. by B842. St. Columba said to have landed here on his first mission to Scotland.

**Saddell Abbey.** 10 m. N. by B842. Cistercian Abbey (ruins) founded c. 1200. Somerled, a lord of the Isles, buried here.

**Carradale House Gardens.** 14 m. N. by B842. *Apr. to Sept. 2-*

*5 daily*. A must for those with green fingers! Fine show, in season, of rhododendrons and azaleas. Forest walks.

See also SOUTHEND, MULL OF KINTYRE (view).

**CASTLE DOUGLAS,** Dumf. and Gall.   3,500   E.C. Thurs.
18 m. S.W. of Dumfries by A75; 10 m. N.E. of Kirkcudbright by A711/A75.

*i* Markethill (0556) 2611

Prosperous little town lying adjacent to delightful Carlingwark Loch where dugout canoes and other relics of past times have been found. Important farming centre.

w **Threave Castle. D.E.** 1½ m. W. off A75 by unclass. road. *Apr. to Sept. 9.30-7 weekdays, 2-7 Sun; Oct. to Mar. 9.30-4 weekdays, 2-4 Sun.* Set on island in R. Dee. Built 1369-1390 by 3rd Earl of Douglas. For time stronghold of Black Douglases. Surrendered to James II (1455). Oldest of all tower-houses.

**Threave Gardens/Visitor Centre. N.T.S.** 2 m. S. off A75. *Open 9 - sunset/9 - 5 (for walled gardens etc.).* Over 600 acres. Peat, rock and water gardens. Go there in Apr. or May for outstanding show of daffodils.

**Mote of Urr. D.E.** 5 m. N.E. off B.794. Circular mound with deep trench surrounding. Saxon/early Norman fortification.

**Orchardton Tower. D.E.** 6 m. S.E. off A711. *9.30-7 weekdays, 2-7 Sun.* Rare example of circular tower-house (mid 15th c.).

See also DALBEATTIE, NEW GALLOWAY/DALRY.

**CERES,** Fife   677
2½ m. S.E. of Cupar by A.91/B.939; 12 m. S.W. of St. Andrews by B.939.

*i* (St. Andrews 12 m.) (0334) 72021.

Particularly attractive little village with some old cottages and a delightful green complete with tiny burn. In the parish church is a mausoleum to the Earls of Crawford.

**Fife Folk Museum.** Well worth visiting.
*Apr. to end Oct., 2-5 ex. Tues.; Sun. 3-6 (ex. Oct. 2-5).*

**Bishop's Bridge.** Hump-backed, dates from medieval times.

**Ceres Highland Games.** *June.*

**COLDSTREAM,** Borders   1,000   E.C. Thurs.
15 m. S.W. of Berwick-upon-Tweed by A698; 9 m. N.E. of Kelso by A698.

*i* Henderson Park (0890) 2607.

Small border town on N. bank of Tweed. Across river lies England. Ford carried many invading armies into Scotland, notably Edward I in 1296. Coldstream Guards regiment raised near here in 1659.

**The Hirsel.** Seat of the Douglas-Home family. Grounds only open (free, except when fund-raising for Scotland's Gardens Scheme).

**Union Suspension Bridge.** 11 m. N.E. by unclass. road. First suspension bridge of its type in Britain. Built 1820.

**Coldstream Annual Civic Week.** *August.*

See also NORHAM, FLODDEN FIELD (both England).

**CRAIL,** Fife    1,000    E.C. Wed.
10 m. S.E. of St. Andrews by A918; 10 m. N.E. of Elie by A917.

One of the picturesque East Neuk fishing villages of Fife. An artist's paradise with gay cottages, narrow streets and harbour brimful of character.

**Tolbooth.** Dates from early 16th c. with unusual fish weathervane. Nearby is Collegiate Church of St. Mary founded 1517. John Knox preached here at beginning of Reformation.

**Scottish Fisheries Museum.** Anstruther. 4 m. S.W. by A917. *Apr. to Oct. 10-12.30, 2-6 weekdays; 2-5 Sun. Nov. to Mar. 2.30-4.30 daily, except Tues.* Everything to do with fishing, fisherfolk and the sea. Aquarium. Reference library.

**Kellie Castle.** N.T.S. 6 m. S.W. by A912. *Apr. to Sept. 2-6 daily, except Mon. and Tues. Gardens open 10-5 daily, Easter to Sept.* Oldest part dates to 14th c. Good example of 16th c. architecture. Outstanding plasterwork and panelling. Gardens extend to 16 acres.

**Church of St. Monan.** St. Monance. *All reasonable times.* 8 m. S.W. by A917. Built by David II. Place of worship for over 600 yrs. Interior has groined roof. Notable are the decorated windows.

**Alexander Selkirk's birthplace.** Lower Largo. 16 m. S.E. by A.917/A.921. The prototype of Robinson Crusoe was born here (1676). See statue of Crusoe.

See also ELIE, PITTENWEEM, LUNDIN LINKS.

**CRIEFF,** Tayside    6,000    E.C. Wed.
17 m. W. of Perth by A85; 22 m. N. of Stirling by A9/A822.
*i* James Sq. (0764) 2578.

One of Scotland's best loved inland resorts. Excellent touring centre for Strathearn.

A unique Museum dedicated to Scottish
Fisherfolk and their Great Industry

# THE SCOTTISH FISHERIES
# MUSEUM AND AQUARIUM

is situated at the head of the ancient, but
still active fishing harbour of ANSTRUTHER
at the heart of the beautiful harbours of the
EAST NEUK OF FIFE
on the north shores of the Firth of Forth.
The Museum is housed in a group of
16th-19th Century buildings surrounding
an attractive cobbled courtyard in which
actual fishing-yawls are on display. Two
70-foot sail fishing-boats are being restored
in the harbour adjacent to the Museum.

TEAROOM                              GIFT SHOP
            TOURIST INFORMATION

*OPEN ALL THE YEAR ROUND*
Apr-Oct:          1000-1230 & 1400-1800 hrs,
                          Sundays 1400-1700 hrs.
Nov-Mar.      1400-1700 hrs every day except
       Tuesdays, Xmas Day and New Year's Day.
ADMISSION:              50p, Senior Citizens &
                                    Children, 25p.
Reduced rates for pre-arranged party visits

For details telephone ANSTRUTHER 310628

🐘 **Strathearn Glass Works.** Glass-making is a local industry and
w visitors are made welcome.

**Mercat (Market) Cross.** Dates from 10th c. bears Celtic
design.

🐘 **Museum of Scottish Tartans.** Comrie. 6 m. W. by A85. *All*
w *year 9-6 daily.* Well set-out display of over 1,300 tartans and
other allied exhibits. Claimed to be largest in existence.
Demonstrations of weaving.

⚹ **Dunmore Hill.** 1 m. N. of Comrie (see above). Magnificent
views of surrounding country.

**Drummond Castle Gardens.** 3 m. S. off A822. *Apr. to Sept.
2-6 (Wed. and Sat.).* Formally laid-out Italian-style gardens.
Of interest is multiple sundial dating from 1630.

🐘 **Innerpeffray Library.** 4 m. S.E. by B8062. Founded 1691, is
oldest public library in Scotland.

. **Muthill Church and Tower. D.E.** 4 m. S. by A822. Ruin of
15th c. church. Tower (type peculiar to this area of Scotland)
dates from 12th c.

**Abercairny Gardens.** 4 m. E. off A85. *Apr. to Sept. dawn 'till
dusk (Wed.).* Splendidly kept grounds with fine blooms
⚹ a-plenty. Excellent views.

**Crieff Highland Gathering.** *August.*

See also SMA' GLEN, AMULREE, GLEN TURRET.

**CUMBRAE (Great),** Strathclyde     1,000     E.C. Wed.
Island in Firth of Clyde. Reached by car/passenger ferry from
Largs (10 mins.)

Favourite little island for those wishing "away from it all".
Paradise for cyclists who do the round the island trip (12 m.)
as a matter of course. Millport is principle township and
offers a fair beach, fishing and sailing.

🐘 **Scottish Marine Biological Station.** N.E. of Millport by A860.
Interesting museum and aquarium.

**Fintry Bay.** 'Over the hill' from Millport. Best sand beach on
island.

See also LITTLE CUMBRAE (boat hires from Millport).

**CUPAR,** Fife     7,000     E.C. Thurs.
20 m. N.E. of Kinross by A91; 10 m. W. of St. Andrews by
A91.

Prosperous town rightly described as 'dignified royal burgh
with many fine houses'. Rail station on main Aberdeen -
Edinburgh line.

**Scotstarvit Tower. D.E.** 3 m. S. off A916. *Apr. to Sept.*
*9.30-7 weekdays, 2-7 Sun; Oct. to Mar. 9.30-4 weekdays, 2-4*
*Sun.* Dates from 1579. Splendid views of surrounding
countryside.

**Hill of Tarvit.** 2 m. S. by A916. Mansion of 1696 open *May to*
*Sept. 2-6 Wed. and Sun.* Has fine collection of furniture,
tapestry, porcelain, paintings. Gardens **N.T.S.** *Open all*
*reasonable times.*

**Fife Folk Museum.** Ceres. 3 m. S.E. by unclass. road. *Apr. to*
*Oct. 2-5 weekdays (ex. Tues. 3-6 Sun. ex. Oct. when 2-5).*
Depicts history of Fife in domestic and agricultural sense. See
also Ceres Church.

w **Lindores Abbey. D.E.** Newburgh. 10 m. N.W. by A913. *All*
*reasonable times.* Founded 1191 by Benedictines. Once an
important religious community of Fife. Now, alas, only
remains. 4 m. S.W. of Abbey is Abernethy Round Tower
**D.E.** 11th c. (see Brechin and Perth).

**Falkland Palace. N.T.S.** 10 m. S.W. by A92/A912. *End Mar.*
*to mid-Oct. 10-6 weekdays, 2-4 Sun.* Built by James IV and V
from 1500-1542. One time seat of Scottish court and a great
'favourite' with Mary, Queen of Scots. Fine 17th c. Flemish
tapestries. Attractive gardens. Royal tennis court dates from
1539.

**Newburgh Highland Games.** *June.*

See also DAIRSIE, DURA DEN, WORMIT/NEWPORT
(TAY BRIDGES).

**DALKEITH,** Lothian      10,000      E.C. Tues.
7 m. S.E. of Edinburgh by A68; 10 m. S.W. of Haddington
by A68/A6093.
Somewhat industrialised town whose environs offer much of
interest to would-be visitors.

**Dalkeith Park.** *Daily from 11 a.m. Mid Apr./Sept.* Delightful
walks skirt R. Esk in grounds of Dalkeith Palace.

w **Inveresk Lodge Garden. N.T.S.** 4 m. N. by A6094. *All year*
*10-4.30 Mon. to Fri. 2-5 Sun. May/Sept.* Like other N.T.S.
garden properties well laid-out and pleasing to the eye.

w **Crichton Castle. D.E.** 7 m. S.E. by A68/B6367. *Apr. to Sept.*
*9.30-7 weekdays, 2-7 Sun; Oct. to Mar. 9.30-4 weekdays, 2-4*
*Sun. Note: Closed Fri. Oct.-May.* Ruins date from about 16th
c. Started as tower-house but became elaborate castle after
many additions. High wall with diamond bosses is worthy of
note.

**Prestongrange Beam Pumping Engine.** 5 m. N. by A6094 (W.

41

of Prestonpans). For viewing apply Prestongrange Brickworks office. Victorian engine dating from 1874, in constant use, for 80 yrs. Used in coal-mining which was hereabouts first begun in Britain.

🐾 **Seton Collegiate Church. D.E.** Route for Prestongrange (see above) thence 3 m. E. by A198. *Apr. to Sept. 9.30-7 weekdays, 2-7 Sun; Oct. to Mar. 9.30-4 weekdays, 2-4 Sun.* Dates from 15th-16th c. Noteworthy is the vaulted chancel and apse.

🐾 **Rosslyn Chapel** (sometimes 'Roslin'). 4 m. S.W. by A6094 and unclass. road. *Easter to Oct. 10-1, 2-5 daily (ex. Sun.).* 15th c. chapel regarded as possibly Scotland's loveliest. Much intricate sculpture. Prentice Pillar is justifiably famous.

See also PRESTON, MUSSELBURGH, NEWBATTLE.

**DINGWALL,** Highland     4,500     E.C. Thurs.
21 m. N.W. of Inverness by A9; 26 m. S.W. of Tain by A9.

*i* Strathpeffer (5 m.) The Square (099 72) 415.

Bustling town at head of Cromarty Firth. Good centre for exploring Muir of Ord and Beauly areas to S. and remote but breathtaking scenery around Achnasheen to W. Made royal burgh by Alexander II in 1226. Birthplace of Macbeth.

w **Beauly Priory, D.E.** 9 m. S. by A9. *Apr. to Sept. 9.30-7 weekdays, 2-7 Sun., Oct. to Mar. 9.30-4 weekdays, 2-4 Sun.* Founded c. 1230 for French Valliscaulian monks. Beauly means 'beautiful place', French beau lieu. The triangular windows and window arcading (chancel) are noteworthy.

**Strathpeffer.** 5 m. W. by A834. Since 18th c. a spa resort with sulphur and chalybeate springs. No pump room nowadays but waters still taken. Ben Wyvis (3429 ft.) dominates the town. Highland Gathering annually in Aug.

**Muir of Ord.** 7 m. S. by A9. Strathconan Games. *July.* Country Show. *Aug.*

⟋ **Struie Hill.** Past Evanton, 6 m. N.E. by A9, take A836.
🜨 Superlative views up and down coast. Particularly fine from Struie Hill (1218 ft.) looking north.

**Dingwall Highland Gathering.** *July.*

See also GARVE/STRATH CONON, STRATH GLASS.

**DORNOCH,** Highland     1,000     E.C. Thurs.
41 m. N.E. of Dingwall by A9/A836/A949; 22 m. S.E. of Lairg by A839/A9/B9168.

*i* The Square (086 281) 400.

Considered by many the most pleasant town in N. Scotland.

Splendid beach, two good golf courses and crystal clear air. Ancient cathedral.

**Dornoch Cathedral.** *Open all reasonable times.* Dates from 1244; destroyed by fire in 1570 it was later restored for Duchess of Sutherland (1837). Further restoration in 1924 revealed fine 13th c. stonework.

**Witch's Stone.** Marks spot where last witch in Scotland was burnt (1722).

**Dunrobin Castle.** Golspie. 12 m. N.E. off A9. Magnificently set in natural terrace overlooking sea. 13th c. seat of Earls of Sutherland now owned by the Countess. Interesting old keep. Fine tapestries and paintings. Gardens well laid out in 17th c. French style. Tea room Gift shop. *Mid-May to mid-Sept., Mon.-Sat. 10.30-5.30; Sun. 1-5.30.*

**Dornoch Highland Gathering.** *August.*

See also SPINNINGDALE, ROGART, GOLSPIE, BRORA.

**DOUNE,** Central 741 E.C. Wed.
9 m. N.W. of Stirling and 8 m. S.E. of Callander by A.84.
(Dunblane 4 m.) (0786) 824428.

Pleasant little place lying just N. of R. Teith. Good accommodation. Fine scenery, especially to W.

**Doune Motor Museum.** 1½ m. N.W. by A.84. Superb collection of vintage and old cars including the second oldest Rolls Royce in world. Most in working order. Cafeteria, souvenir and gift shop. Free parking. *Apr.-Oct., 10-6, daily.*

*ex. Apr., May, Sept., Oct., when 10-4.30.*
**See ad at back.**

**Doune Castle. D.E.** ½ m. S. of village. Dates from 14th c. One of best preserved medieval castles in Scotland. Two fine towers with hall in between. Panoramic views over R. Teith. *Enquire locally for opening times.*

**Doune Motor Racing Hill Climb.** *Annually in April, June, Sept.*

**DRUMNADROCHIT,** Highland    500
15 m. S.W. of Inverness by A82.

On N. shore of Loch Ness. Quiet little place with strange-sounding name. From hereabouts a number of sightings of the 'Monster' have been made. Have your camera handy!

W **Urquhart Castle. D.E.** 2 m. S.E. by A82. *Apr. to Sept. 9.30-7 weekdays, 2-7 Sun.; Oct. to Mar. 9.30-4 weekdays, 2-4 Sun.* Dates back to 1200. Now an extensive ruin, it changed hands many times in wars of Bruce. Blown up in 1692 to forestall Jacobite intruders. Claim made that buried treasure lies beneath vaults.

**Glenurquhart Highland Games.** *August.*

See also GLEN URQUHART, INVERMORISTON, GLEN MORISTON.

**DUMBARTON,** Strathclyde    25,000    E.C. Wed.
15 m. N.W. of Glasgow by A82/A814; 5 m. S. of Balloch (Loch Lomond) by A813 (slip road).

Basically a rather unattractive town at mouth of R. Leven. One time (5th c.) ancient capital of kingdom of Strathclyde a fact which it still boasts at its main approaches. Town centre has recently undergone considerable modernisation and a goodish shopping precinct has resulted. Helensburgh 8 m. N.W. was birthplace of John Logie Baird, pioneer of television.

**Dumbarton Castle. D.E.** *Apr. to Sept. 9.30-7 weekdays, 2-7 Sun.; Oct. to Mar. 9.30-4 weekdays, 2-4 Sun.* Perched atop Dumbarton Rock (240 ft.) this was a royal castle until the Middle Ages. Mary, Queen of Scots left here for France in 1548, when five years old. See sundial gifted by her to town; also 12th c. gateway. Fine panoramic views made more interesting by good indicator plate.

**Hill House, Helensburgh.** 8 m. N.W. by A814. *1-8 Tues., Thurs. and Fri.; 9-5 Wed. and Sun.; 12-5 Sat.* Built 1902 by Charles Rennie Mackintosh, the famous Glasgow architect. Good examples of Mackintosh furniture, etc.

**Glenarn Gardens. Rhu.** 10 m. N.W. by A814. *Mar. to Aug. 9-9 daily.* Rhododendrons, azaleas, magnolias . . . and much more.

See also GLEN FRUIN, WHISTLEFIELD (View), PORTIN-CAPLE (view), KILCREGGAN.


**DUMFRIES,** Dumf. and Gall.      29,500      E.C. Thurs.
24 m. W. of Gretna (border) by A75; 13 m. W. of Lockerbie by A709.

*i* Whitesands (0387) 3862.

Much associated with Robert Burns' latter years. A prosperous town on R. Nith which periodically bursts its banks and causes flooding problems around the Whitesands. Some good hotels. Ideal centre for exploring Nithsdale and Annandale.

**Burns' House/Mausoleum.** *House: Apr. to Sept. 10-1, 2-7
W Mon./Fri., 2-7 Sun. Oct. to Mar. 10-12 Mon./Fri. 2-5 Sun.*
Burns died here on July 21, 1796. Relics, manuscripts, etc. on view. Mausoleum (viewed from outside) contains Burns' remains and those of his family.

**Globe Inn.** (off High St.). One of Burns' favourite drinking
W places. Still a flourishing pub today.

**Midsteeple** (town centre). Dates from 1707, formerly the tolbooth. Has interesting plan depicting the town in Burns' time.

W **Lincluden College/Abbey. D.E.** 1 m. N. off A76. *Apr. to Sept. 9.30-7 weekdays, 2-7 Sun.; Oct. to Mar. 9.30-4 week-days, 2-4 Sun.* Founded in 12th c. for Benedictine nuns. Little now remains though worthy of attention is heraldic adornment at entry to choir and tomb (1430) of Princess Margaret, daughter of Robert III.

**Ellisland Farm.** 7 m. N.W. off A76. Robert Burns rather un-successfully farmed here for three years (1788/91). Composed Tam o'Shanter and Auld Lang Syne, probably his best known poems. From here he moved to Dumfries and became an exciseman.

W **Sweetheart Abbey. D.E.** 8 m. S. by A710. *Apr. to Sept. 9.30-7 weekdays, 2-7 Sun.; Oct. to Mar. 9.30-4 weekdays, 2-4 Sun.* Built by Devorgilla Balliol (1273) who also founded Balliol College, Oxford. Now a beautiful ruin, 'Sweetheart' is derived from the fact that Devorgilla carried her husband's heart with her for many years. She, with the heart of her betrothed, was buried near the high altar.

**Arbigland** (near Kirkbean). 12 m. S. off A710. *May to Sept. 2-6 Tues., Thurs., Sun.* Extensive woodland. Well laid out

45

formal and water gardens. John Paul Jones, founder of the American navy, was born near here in 1747.

w **Caerlaverock Castle. D.E.** 9 m. S. off B725. *Apr. to Sept. 9.30-7 weekdays, 2-7 Sun; Oct. to Mar. 9.30-4 weekdays, 2-4 Sun.* A Maxwell stronghold dating mainly from 15th c. Has unusual triangular design with round towers. The Renaissance façade is notable. Nearby is an extensive Nature Reserve well known for its wildfowl, etc.

**Guid Nychburris Week.** *June.*

See also LOCHMABEN, LOCKERBIE, GLENKILN, GLENCAPLE.

**DUNBAR,** Lothian     5,000     E.C. Wed.
28 m. E. of Edinburgh by A1/A1087; 30 m. N.W. of Berwick-upon-Tweed by A1/A1087.

*i* Town House, High St. (0368) 63353.

Leading seaside resort with good sand beaches and picturesque harbour overlooked by castle. High levels of sunshine are consistently recorded in this part of Scotland.

**Dunbar Castle.** Now ruins. Mary, Queen of Scots with Bothwell surrendered castle to her rebellious nobles in 1567. Site of Battle of Dunbar (1650), in which Cromwell defeated the Covenanters, is 2 m. distant (nr. Broxburn).

**Town House.** Dates from 17th c. Quaint building with six-sided tower. Claims to be oldest civic building in Scotland (still in regular use).

**Dunglass Collegiate Church. D.E.** 8 m. S.E. off A1. Dates from 1450. Contains much rich detail, especially interior. See nave, choir, transepts. etc.

w **Preston Mill. N.T.S.** 6 m. W. off A1. *Apr. to Sept. 10-12.30, 2-7.30 weekdays, 2-7.30 Sun.; Oct. to Mar. 10-12.30, 2-4.30 weekdays, 2-4.30 Sun.* 17th c. grain water-mill still in working order. Probably oldest in Scotland. Close by is the Phantassie dovecot of traditional Scottish style.

See also EAST LINTON, STENTON, BARNS NESS.

**DUNBLANE,** Central     5,500     E.C. Wed.
6 m. N. of Stirling by A9; 12 m. S.E. of Callander by A84/A820.

*i* Stirling Rd. (0786) 824428.

Pleasant little town of narrow streets and sprinkling of interesting shops. Allan Water is nearby. See riverwalk in springtime when sloping banks are ablaze with daffodils.

**Dunblane Cathedral.** *Apr. to Sept. 9.30-7 weekdays, 2-5 Sun. Oct. to Mar. 9.30-4 weekdays, 2-4 Sun.* Dates from 13th c. Museum has varied collection of historical relics pertaining to Cathedral, Dunblane and environs.

**Keir Gardens.** 2 m. S. off B824. *Apr. to Oct. 2-6 Tues. Wed. Thurs.* Flowering shrubs, yew tree house, water garden etc. Keir House (no adm.) was where Chopin stayed in 1848.

**Sheriffmuir.** 3 m. E. by unclass. road off A9. Site of battle (1715) between Earl of Mar and Duke of Argyll.

**Dunblane Highland Games.** *September.*

See also KIPPEN.


**DUNDEE,** Tayside      181,000      E.C. Wed.
21 m. E. of Perth by A85; 68 m. S. of Aberdeen by A929/ A94; 57 m. N. of Edinburgh by M90 (Forth and Tay bridges).

*i* 16 City Sq. (0382) 23141.

**Weather:** (038 34) 2566.

Third largest city in Scotland after Glasgow and Edinburgh. For long (and still is to some extent) associated with jam, jute and journalism as means of economic prosperity. One time major centre for whaling industry, this has now gone. Extensive modernisation has kept Dundee in line with other major British cities and the splendid 1½ m. Tay road bridge (1966) is the longest span over any river in the country. One mile W. is the rail bridge. Built in 1887 it replaced a former bridge which was blown down in a fierce gale while a train was crossing. The Tay Bridge disaster of 1879 resulted in the deaths of 75 people. Caird Hall, one of many fine buildings, has been acclaimed as "accoustically perfect" and attracts some of the large touring orchestras (eg. Hallé) and many international artists of world repute.

**Dundee City Museum and Art Gallery.** Albert Sq. *All year
W 10-5.30 weekdays.* Houses many exhibits on Old Dundee, its shipping and industry. Fine collection of paintings — Flemish, Dutch, French and British schools.

**The Howff** (Reform St./Meadowside.) For 300 yrs. (to 1857) the city's chief burying ground. Gifted to the town by Mary, Queen of Scots, it has many quaint gravestones.

**Old Steeple/Tower of St. Mary.** (off City Sq.) *10-1, 2-dusk
W Mon./Thurs. and Sat.* The most notable building in Dundee. 156 ft. high and dates from 15th c. Within Scotland, the largest and finest of its kind.

**H.M.S. 'Unicorn'.** Dundee Harbour. A 46-gun Royal Navy

frigate launched in 1824. Oldest remaining British-built warship still afloat.

**Camperdown Park.** Kingsway West. (N.W. of city centre). Extends to 600 acres. Nature trail, many rare trees and, W nearby, the Spalding Golf Museum — a must for all lovers of the sport.

**Dundee Law** (north of city centre). Highest point in the city (571 ft.). Was once a volcano. Fine panoramic views extend E. from Budden Ness (Tay estuary) and W. across the Carse of Gowrie towards Perth.

**Claypotts Castle. D.E.** 4 m. E. by A930. Built between 1569-88. One of Scotland's most intact turreted tower-houses. See crow-stepped gables.

**Dundee Highland Games.** *July.*
See also MONIFIETH, CARNOUSTIE.

**DUNFERMLINE,** Fife        53,500        E.C. Wed.
17 m. N.W. of Edinburgh by A90 (Forth bridge); 30 m. S. of Perth by M90/A907.

*i* Glen Bridge Car Park (0383) 20999.

Favourite residence of early Scottish kings. Once capital of Scotland. Has important historic remains. Andrew Carnegie, the philanthropist who died in 1919, was native of town. Much of his great wealth went towards the prosperity of Dunfermline. Town once famed for its linen and damask. Alas, man-made fibres have now largely taken over.

**Dunfermline Abbey.** *Apr. to Sept. 9.30-7 weekdays, 2-7 Sun,; Oct. to Mar. 9.30-4 weekdays, 2-4 Sun.* (N.B. closed on Suns. during services). Founded in 11th c. by King Malcolm (Canmore). Norman nave of 1150 said to be finest of its period in Scotland. Seven Scottish kings are buried here, among them Alexander I, David I and Robert Bruce. He, the last buried, (1329) was interred in the choir, the spot being marked by a brass plate. Among those born in the adjacent royal Palace (largely ruins) was Charles I in 1600.

**Andrew Carnegie's Cottage.** Moodie St. *Apr. to Sept. 11-1* W *and 2-7 weekdays, 2-6 Sun.; Oct. to Mar. as above but closes 5 p.m.* Andrew Carnegie born here in 1835. The cottage is now a museum.

**Dunfermline Museum.** Viewfield. *Apr. to Sept. 11-6 Mon.* W *and Wed./Sat. 1-6 Sun.; Oct. to Mar. 11-5 Wed./Sat. 1-5 Sun.* Depicts the local history of the town. Exhibits of linen and damask articles are noteworthy.

**Pittencrieff Park.** Bequeathed to the town by Carnegie in

1903. Superb formal gardens. Aviary, nature trail, children's play areas, maze, costume gallery, etc. Sometimes regarded a one of the showpieces of Scotland.

**Inchcolm Abbey. D.E.** (island in Firth of Forth reached from Aberdour 8 m. E. by B916/A92 . . . boat hires durin summer). *Apr. to Sept. 9.30-7 weekdays; 2-7 Sun.* Founde 1123 by Alexander I. Well preserved remains, especiall octagonal chapter-house. Wall paintings in choir can still b seen.

**Culross Palace. D.E.** 8 m. W. by A994. *Apr. to Sept. 9.30- weekdays; 2-7 Sun.; Oct. to Mar. 9.30-4 weekdays, 2-4 Sur.* Late 16th c. town mansion. Features are crow-stepped gable and pantiled roofs. Some rooms are painted with religiou scenes, the best being in W. wing. Of the 13th c. Culros Abbey only the choir remains.

**The 'Study' Culross. N.T.S.** (directions as above). *Mar. t w Oct. 10-12.30, 2-7 weekdays, 2-5 Sun.; Nov. to Feb. 10-12.30 2-4 Sat. 2-4 Sun.* An L-plan house of late 16th c. The name derives from one small room at the top of its tower. Note worthy is the panelled Culross Room. Nearby the 'Ark' and 'Nunnery' are two other 17th c. buildings under N.T.S. care

See also LIMEKILNS, INVERKEITHING, KINGHORN.

**DUNKELD,** Tayside     1,000     E.C. Thurs.
15 m. N.W. of Perth by A9; 12 m. S.E. of Pitlochry by A9.

*i* The Cross (035 02) 460.

Often linked with neighbouring Birnam. Delightfully situated 'city' (on account of Cathedral) lying in wooded valley on R Tay. Good touring centre for one of most attractive areas o Scotland. Salmon fishing on famous Tay between here and Stanley has yielded the heaviest rod-caught fish in Britain though understandably it is very expensive.

**Dunkeld Cathedral. D.E.** *Apr. to Sept. 9.30-7 weekdays, 2-. Sun.; Oct. to Mar. 9.30-4 weekdays, 2-4 Sun.* Founded 9th c Choir of 14th c. now used as parish church. Fine windov tracery on nave. See wall paintings on massive tower.

**Little Houses. N.T.S.** (no adm.). Privately occupied dwelling dating from c. 1690. Since 1950 carefully restored by Trus and preserved for posterity.

**Tay Bridge.** Built by Telford in 1809. A fine bridge linkin, Dunkeld with Birnam.

**The Hermitage. N.T.S.** 2 m. W. off A9. A rotunda, summer house built in 1758 by a Duke of Atholl. Originally centre piece of wild garden. Fine woodlands with nature trail and

49

nearby the picturesque R. Braan. If lucky you'll see wild cat, capercailzie and badgers.

**Loch of the Lowes.** 2 m. N.E. off A923. Bird sanctuary owned by Scottish Wildlife Trust. Visitor centre. Ospreys nest in area and can be observed from hide.

See also STRATH BRAAN, CAPUTH.

**DUNOON,** Strathclyde    9,000    E.C. Wed.
76 m. W. of Glasgow by A82/A815 (via Rest and be Thankful). 26 m. W. of Glasgow by M8/A8 to Gourock thence ferry. (20 mins.).

*i* Pier Esplanade (0369) 3785.

Well situated town with splendid views of Firth of Clyde. Steamer cruises a-plenty. Magnificent backcloth of hills stretching N. to L. Eck and Argyll Forest Park and W. to Glendaruel, Colintraive and Tighnabruaich. Town itself somewhat disappointing to first-time visitors. This ''Jewel of Cowal'' is, however, striving hard to maintain and, indeed, to increase its undoubted charm and appeal.

**Dunoon Ceramics.** Hamilton St. Specialises in high-quality stone-ware, coffee mugs and tableware. Guided tours of factory. Seconds shop and craft shop. Refreshments. *Daily, 9.30-4.30.*

**Cowal Highland Gathering.** *(last Fri. and Sat. in Aug.).* Dunoon still attracts a host of visitors during this famous Gathering. Its March of 1,000 Pipers, a colourful-event possibly without rival, culminates the proceedings.

**'Highland Mary' Statue.** (adjacent to pier). Burns' sweetheart Mary Campbell is here commemorated. The nearby **Morag's Fairy Glen** (delightful waterfalls) is well worth the climb out of town.

**Younger Botanic Garden.** 7 m. N.W. by A815. *Apr. to Oct. 10-6 daily.* Woodland gardens, flowering trees and shrubs. The avenue of sequois is noteworthy.

**Tighnabruaich.** 25 m. W. by A885/B836/A8003. No visitor to Dunoon should miss the superb views of L. Striven, L. Riddon and Kyles of Bute which this route offers.

See also KILMUN, ARDENTINNY, STRACHUR, INNELLAN.

**DUNS,** Borders.    2,000    E.C. Wed.
13 m. N. of Coldstream by A6112; 47 m. S.E. of Edinburgh by A68/A697/A6105.

County town of Berwickshire prior to regionalisation in 1975.

# Manderston

## "The finest Edwardian House in the classical style in Britain"

*The home of Mr. and Mrs. Adrian Palmer.*

The house and the buildings of Manderston, together with the park and gardens form an extraordinary ensemble which is unique in Britain.

Here you will see not only a great classical house with fine rooms and decoration, but also:

Buxley Farm with its astounding marble dairy. The stables with magnificent teak stalls and solid brass posts.

The lake, woodland garden and formal gardens. Before you leave, you may care to look in the gift shop or sample the cream teas served in the tea room.

## OPEN

May 18th - 21st September
Thursdays & Sundays
2 - 5.30 p.m.
Also the Bank Holiday
Mondays of May 26th and
August 25th.
Parties at any time by
appointment.

Good angling centre for nearby Whiteadder and Blackadder Waters.

🐦 **Manderston.** 1½ m. E. of A.6105. Claims to be the finest Edwardian House in the classical style in Britain. Many fine rooms on views with decoration in Adam manner. Lake, stables, woodland and formal gardens. *May 18 to Sept. 21, Thur. & Sun. 2-5.30.*

🐦 **Jim Clark Museum.** *10-1, 2-5, 6-8 Mon./Sat. 2-8 Sun.* The
w world motor racing champion (killed 1966) was a native of town. Many trophies won during his reign are displayed.

**Edin's Hall Broch. D.E.** 4 m. N. off A6112. Defensive tower of iron age Scotland. Only nine others in south Scotland. The thick base wall stands almost 5 ft. high.

**Foulden Old Tithe Barn. D.E.** 9 m. N.E. by A6105. Viewed from roadside. Two-storeyed building with outside stair and gables.

**Duns Summer Festival and Common Riding.** *July.*

See also CHIRNSIDE, EDROM, GREENLAW, GORDON, ABBEY ST. BATHANS.

**DURNESS,** Highland     500     E.C. Sat. (out of season). 56 m. N.W. of Lairg by A838; 37 m. N.W. of Tongue by A838.

𝑙 Information Centre (097 181) 259.

Friendly little village near extreme N.W. tip of Scottish mainland. An angler's paradise famed for its trout lochs and Dionard river (salmon). There is much of interest in the area and the magnificent sand beaches are usually deserted.

**Durness Old Church. D.E.** ½ m. W. by unclass road. Built 1619, now a roofless ruin. Nearby an obelisk commemorates the Gaelic poet Rob Donn (1740-78).

🐦 **Balnakeil Craft Village.** (directions as above). On site of
w former R.A.F. camp now transformed into busy little self-supporting community making and selling all manner of things.

🐦 **Smoo Caves.** 2 m. E. by A838. Comprises of three huge caves running deep into limestone cliffs. First cave measures about 200 ft. (lengthwise) by 120 ft. high (easily reached from beach). Seek local advice on exploration of interior caves.

🦌 **Cape Wrath.** 13 m. W. by unclass. road via Keoldale ferry (pass. only). Mini-bus service (May - end Sept.) connects ferry on W. side Kyle of Durness for Cape Wrath lighthouse visit. Views seaward include Orkney, 60 m. N.E. and Butt of Lewis, 45 m. W.

**Durness Highland Gathering.** *July.*

See also LOCH ERIBOLL, KINLOCHBERVIE, SAND-WOOD BAY, SCOURIE.

**EDINBURGH,** Lothian    450,000    E.C. varies in suburbs. 45 m. E. of Glasgow by A8/M8; 37 m. S.E. of Stirling by A9/M9.

*i* 5 Waverley Bridge (031) 226 6591; 225 5801; 332 2433.

**Weather:** (031) 246 8091.

Capital of Scotland sometimes called "Athens of the North" on account of its thoughtful planning and many fine buildings. Two aspects of this city — the old and new — are soon apparent to would-be sightseers. Edinburgh Castle and Royal Mile are steeped in history and not surprisingly attract tourists from all over world. New Edinburgh, basically Georgian, lies to N. of world-famous Princes St. — particularly attractive due to its open aspect over the Gardens to the silhouetted Castle above. Edinburgh too is a leading cultural centre and justly boasts its annual International Festival of Music and Drama while, running concurrently, is the Military Tattoo on the Castle Esplanade, the Film Festival and the ever popular Fringe Festival which embraces a Children's Section, Dance and Mime, Music and Verse and many other events. But Edinburgh has much more to offer . . . visit Murrayfield when Scotland are hosts to England, Wales, Ireland or France in a Rugby Union International match. See the vast Meadowbank Sports Centre (London Rd.), venue for 1970 Commonwealth Games, have a dip in the splendid Royal Commonwealth Pool (Dalkeith Rd.) climb the 800 ft. 'Arthur's Seat' for possibly best panoramic views of city and environs. Take the kiddies to the fine zoo at Corstorphine. Pressed for time? Enjoy a city tour by luxury coach from Waverley Bridge. Edinburgh has all this and more . . . much more.

**Edinburgh Castle. D.E.** W. end of Royal Mile. *May to Oct. 9.30-6 weekdays, 11-6 Sun.; Nov. to Apr. 9.30-5.15 weekdays, 12.30-4.30 Sun.* Visited by upwards of 800,000 persons annually. St. Margaret's Chapel, one of oldest buildings in Edinburgh, built by Queen Margaret c. 1076. Scottish Nat. War Museum (1927) houses Gallery of Honour devoted to famous regiments. Military Museum contains Scotland's Regalia (Crown jewels). Queen Mary's Apartments have some fine furniture, pictures and relics (akin to Jacobites). The 15th c. cannon Mons Meg, possibly of Belgian origin is on King's Bastion. If in doubt about correct time you can check your watch with 1 o'clock gun which has

# THE EDINBURGH WAX MUSEUM

presents

# A FESTIVAL OF WAX

*Beautifully costumed models*
*depict*
*exciting scenes from Scotland's Past*

*Children of all ages will love*

# 'NEVER NEVER' LAND

and

Visit — if you dare

the

# 'CHAMBER OF HORRORS'

Open seven days a week. Special Group Rates
142, High Street, Edinburgh — 031-226-4445

been fired regularly (except for war years) since 1861.

🦅 **Camera Obscura.** Castle Hill. *Mid-Mar. to mid-Oct. 10-6 weekdays, 12.30 - 6 Sun.* Darkened room with screen on which is cleverly projected image of immediate surroundings.

🎎 **Museum of Childhood.** Royal Mile. *June to Sept. 10-6 weekdays, Oct. to May 10-5 weekdays. (Suns. during Festival only).* Toys, dolls and everything of interest to young folk.

🎎 **Wax Museum.** Royal Mile.
W     Like a mini Madame Tussaud's but with a distinctively Scottish flavour to its characters. Children will love it all . . . even, perhaps, the Chamber of Horrors!
*Apr. to Sept. Daily, 10-7; Oct.-Mar., daily 10-5.*

🦅 **Palace of Holyroodhouse. D.E.** Foot of Royal Mile. *May to*
W *Oct. 9-30-6 weekdays, 11-6 Sun.; Nov. Apr. 9.30-5.15 weekdays, 12.30-4.30 Sun.* Closed during all Royal and State visits. Queen's official residence while in Scotland, apart from Balmoral (q.v.). Palace built c. 1500 by James IV and James V. Mary, Queen of Scots lived here for six yrs. met John Knox and married Bothwell. The Young Pretender, Prince Charles Edward Stuart, held court in 1745. Interesting tapestries and paintings in State apartments. Picture Gallery contains portraits of 111 Scottish kings. (See also Holyrood Abbey.)

🦅 **St. Giles High Kirk.** Royal Mile. *10-5 weekdays.* Present structure dates from late 15th c. Conspicuous square central tower. John Knox was minister here (1559-72). Interior rightly described as dignified and beautiful. See Thistle Chapel.

🦅 **John Knox House.** Royal Mile. *10-5 weekdays.* Lower part of
W house dates from c. 1473 — remainder from early 17th c. No firm evidence that Knox actually lived here though much interesting material akin to the preacher is on view. Thought by many to be Edinburgh's most attractive old house.

🦅 **Lady Stair's House.** Royal Mile. *10-5 weekdays.* Early 17th c.
W house worth seeing while on this famous old street. Now a museum given over to Scotland's three great literary geniuses, Burns, Scott and Stevenson.

🦅 **Canongate Tolbooth.** Royal Mile. *June to Sept. 10-6 week-*
W *days; Oct. to May 10-5 weekdays.* Part of the City Museum (Huntly House), this turreted tower dates from 1591. Has an interesting collection of Highland dress and tartans. Nearby is Canongate Kirk (1688).

🦅 **Georgian House. N.T.S.** 7 Charlotte Square. *Easter to mid-*
W *Oct. 10-5 weekdays, 2-5 Sun.; mid-Oct. to Easter 10-5 Sat.; 2-5 Sun.* Sumptuously furnished in typical Georgian style this splendidly designed Adams house (c. 1800) is accepted as

forming with Nos. 5 and 6 one of Europe's finest frontages. See also Heriot Row and Moray Place.

**Princes Street.** Well worth the walk from E. to W. (Gardens side) to catch the cosmopolitan aspect of this great city and see some well-known landmarks (Scott Monument, Royal Scottish Academy, National Gallery of Scotland, Floral Clock, St. John's and St. Cuthbert's Churches, Scottish American and Royal Scots Greys memorials). N. side of Princes St. has almost continuous line of departmental chain stores and shops though sadly the once elegant buildings offering high class merchandise have largely disappeared.

**Edinburgh Zoo.** Corstorphine Rd. 4 m. W. by A8. *Apr. to Sept. 9-7 daily; Oct. to Mar. 9-5.* Laid out on hillside this famous zoo rivals the best in Britain. Penguin Parade (mid-afternoon) is worth seeing.

**Hillend Ski Centre.** 5 m. S. off A702. *Daily.* Britain's largest artificial ski-slope. Chairlift, tuition, etc. Magnificent views.

**Royal Botanic Garden.** Inverleith Row (via Hanover St. from city centre). *Summer 9-one hour before sunset weekdays. (Sun. from 11 a.m.). Winter 9-dusk.* Has outstanding rock garden and unique collection of rhododendrons. Interesting plant houses. See also (within grounds) National Gallery of Modern Art.

**Craigmillar Castle. D.E.** 4 m. S.W. by A68. *Apr. to Sept. 9.30 - 7 weekdays, 2 - 7 Sun.; Oct. to Mar. 9.30 - 4 weekdays, 2-4 Sun.* Tower-house c. 1374. Ruins of 14th c. keep. One of Mary, Queen of Scots best loved residences. Here plot laid for Darnley's murder.

**Huntly House.** Royal Mile (142 Canongate). One of city's most important and interesting museums. Contains original copy of 1638 National Covenant. The building, with its fine timbered front, has collections of Edinburgh silver, glass and Scottish pottery plus local history items. *June-Sept., weekdays, 10-6; rest of year, weekdays, 10-5.*

**Laurieston Castle.** 4 m. N.W. near A90. *Apr. to Oct. 11-1 and 2-5 daily (ex. Fri.) Nov. to Mar. 2-4 Sat. and Sun. only.* Dates from c. 1590. Pleasant views over Firth of Forth. Has fine paintings, furniture and Blue John ware.

**Royal Highland Show.** (Ingliston). *June.*

**Edinburgh Highland Games.** *August.*

**Edinburgh International Festival of Music and Drama.** *Late Aug/early Sept.*

See also CRAMOND, DEAN VILLAGE, SWANSTON, DUDDINGSTON, FORTH BRIDGES.

**ELGIN,** Grampian.　　17,500　　E.C. Wed.
67 m. N.W. of Aberdeen by A96; 39 m. N.E. of Inverness by A96.

*i* 17 High St. (0343) 3388.

Often known as the 'Lantern of the North' this bustling town boasts a ruined Cathedral and fine architecture in some of its buildings. There is much of interest nearby and Lossiemouth, a popular seaside resort, is only 5 m. distant.

w **Elgin Cathedral. D.E.** *Apr. to Sept. 9.30-7 weekdays, 2-7 Sun. Oct. to Mar. 9.30-4 weekdays, 2-4 Sun.* Founded 1274. Authorities state that, in 13th c., this was finest Cathedral in Scotland. Today the ruins are still very beautiful. Of special note is the choir and west front.

**Spynie Palace.** 2 m. N. off A941. View from outside. c. 1200. An impressive ruined castle of the bishops of Moray.

🐾 **Pluscarden Abbey.** 6 m. S.W. by B9010 and unclass. road. w *Open all reasonable times.* Originally a Cistercian monastery. Dates from 1230. Nowadays occupied by Benedictine monks striving to restore the well-preserved remains.

**Elgin Highland Games.** *July.*

See also CRAIGELLACHIE, LOSSIEMOUTH, BURGHEAD, FORRES.

**EYEMOUTH,** Borders    2,500    E.C. Thurs.
8 m. N. of Berwick-upon-Tweed by A1/A1107; 50 m. S.E. of
Edinburgh by A1/A1107.

*ℓ* Home Arms Car Park (0390) 50678.

Pleasant little fishing port and popular holiday resort with
lively harbour. Fine coastal scenery. Caves and caverns used
by smugglers in 18th c. can be reached along foreshore.

**Coldingham Priory.** 3 m. N.W. by A1107. *Open all reasonable*
W *times.* Founded c. 1147 it was partly destroyed by Cromwell in
1648. Choir since restored and now forms the parish church,
one of oldest still in use.

**St. Abb's Head.** Route for Coldingham thence B6438 and
coastal path. A paradise for ornithologists. Observation
point. Famous for its bird colonies, notably fulmars.

**Herring Queen Week.** *July.*

See also BURNMOUTH.

**FALKLAND,** Fife    1,000    E.C. Thur.
12 m. N. of Kirkcaldy by A.92/A.912; 3 m. S. of
Auchtermuchty by A.983.

*ℓ* Falkland Palace (N.T.S.) *Mid-Mar. to end Oct.* (033 75) 397.

Small though very interesting Royal Burgh, much visited on
account of its palace. Old world atmosphere with cobbled
streets, attractive little houses plus the palace. Well-stocked
local shop with antiques. Cottage craft centre nearby.

**Falkland Palace. N.T.S.** Built by James IV and V from 1500-
1542. One time seat of Scottish court and great favourite of
Mary, Queen of Scots. 17th c. Flemish tapestries. Attractive
gardens. Royal tennis court (note unusual markings) dates
from 1539. *Mid Apr. to end Oct., weekdays 10-6; Suns. 2-6.
Last adm. 5.15.*

**Kind Kyttock's Kitchen.** Cross Wynd . Home baking at its
best. Lunches and light meals. Tea garden. *Apr. to end Oct.,
daily, 10.30-6. Nov.-March, 10.30-6, weekends only.*

**Lomond Hills.** Minor road to Leslie. Slightly S. of Falkland,
the hills, E. Lomond (1,471 ft.) and W. Lomond (1,713 ft.)
are highest in Fife. Panoramic views from reasonably easily
reached summits.

**FORFAR,** Tayside    11,500    E.C. Thurs.
14 m. N. of Dundee by A929; 15 m. N.W. of Arbroath by
A933/A932.

A busy town with a somewhat old world atmosphere.
Malcolm III said to have held a Parliament here in 1057
though this is uncertain as Cromwell's men destroyed all the

# kind kyttock's kitchen

**TEAROOM** and Art Gallery : Tea Garden

**CROSS WYND**, Falkland, Fife (Tel. 03375 — 477)

*(Opposite The Green — Parking Available)*

### OPEN DAILY FROM 10.30 a.m.

*(Closed Weekdays November — March)*

**HOME BAKING FRESH DAILY : LUNCHES
AFTERNOON TEAS : LIGHT MEALS**

**Morning Coffee/Teas : Hot/Cold Snacks**

*Recommended in Egon Ronay's 'Just A Bite'*

Admitted to membership of the Scottish
Tourist Board's "Taste for Scotland" project.

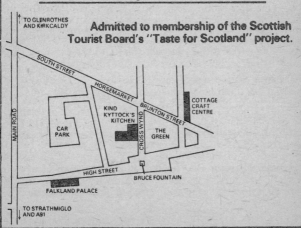

59

town records in 1651. The name Forfar makes one think of its well-known bridies — savoury pasties with a filling of mince and onions. Delicious when hot!

🐦 **Town Hall.** Dates from 1788 and contains some fine old masters and the interesting Forfar 'bridle' or gag — a collar-type device with prong used on those about to be executed.

w **Restenneth Priory. D.E.** 1 m. E. by B9113. *Apr. to Sept. 9.30-7 weekdays, 2-7 Sun,; Oct. to Mar. 9.30-4 weekdays, 2-4 Sun.* Mainly 12th c. Thought to have been founded by David I. Notable is the 15th c. broach spire and the earlier square tower. Priory said to be an offshoot of Jedburgh Abbey.

**Aberlemno Sculptured Stones. D.E.** 5 m. N.E. by B9134. Three stones stand beside the road, all from Pictish times. Of special note is the cross-slab with symbols (8th c.) in the nearby churchyard.

🐦 **Barrie's Birthplace** (Kirriemuir). **N.T.S.** 5 m. N.W. by A926. *Apr. to Oct. 10-12.30, 2-6 weekdays; 2-6 Sun.* Sir James Barrie creator of Peter Pan and the "Thrums" of his novels born here (9 Brechin Rd.) in 1860. Home now a museum with interesting manuscripts, personal possessions, etc. A camera obscura is located near the cemetery in which Barrie was buried (1937).

🐦 **Glamis Castle.** 8 m. S.W. by A928. *May to Sept. 2-5.30 Sun./ Thurs.* In present form dates mainly from 17th c. Childhood home of Queen Elizabeth the Queen Mother. Princess Margaret born here in 1930. Fine collection of furnishings, china and armour. See also (in grounds) the great sundial, 21 ft. in height with 84 dials.

**Angus Folk Museum,** Glamis. **N.T.S.** 5 m. S.W. by A94. *Easter to Sept. 1-6 daily.* Restored cottages (early 19th c.) now house exhibits depicting domestic and agricultural life in the area over period of some 200 years.

**Forfar Highland Games.** *June.*

See also TANNADICE, GLEN CLOVA.

**FORRES,** Grampian     5,500     E.C. Wed.
12 m. W. of Elgin by A96; 11 m. E. of Nairn by A96.

*i* High St. (030 92) 2278.

Pleasant little town near R. Findhorn. Mentioned in Shakespeare's 'Macbeth' regarding King Duncan's court. Cluny Hill, E. of town, offers particularly fine views (see Nelson Monument). The local Falconer Museum has interesting collection of fossils, arrowheads, etc. from the nearby Culbin Sands.

**Suenos Stone. D.E.** 1 m. N.E. by B9011. Remarkable carved pillar 23 ft. high. Early Christian period.

**Nelson Monument** (on Cluny Hill E. of town) offers excellent views of Findhorn Bay and surroundings.

**Witches Stone** (in town). Inscription tells how local witches were once burnt here, having previously been rolled down Cluny Hill in stout barrels through which spikes were driven!

**Kincorth.** 5 m. N.W. by A96 thence unclass. road (signposted). *June, July, Aug. 9-9 Mon./Fri.* Splendid lawns, trees and all that makes for a very fine garden.

See also FINDHORN.

**FORT AUGUSTUS,** Highland     500     E.C. Wed.
34 m. S.W. of Inverness by A82; 32 m. N.E. of Fort William by A82.

*i* Information Centre Car Park (032 03) 367.

Fine touring centre for Loch Ness-side and Great Glen running S.W. to Fort William. A fort built after the Jacobite rising (1715) gave name to the village. Benedictine abbey and boys' boarding school now occupy site. Fort Augustus stands at head of 24 m. long Loch Ness and the Caledonian Canal which here passes through several locks. See General Wade's military roads.

**Fort Augustus Abbey.** Guided tours available. Dates from 1876 though succeeds two older abbeys of 1645 and c. 1100. Visitors are admitted to the church and museum.

**Great Glen Exhibition.** Audio-visual show tells one all about the Glen. Fact or fiction on the Loch Ness 'Monster' is also available. In the great loch itself you may get the proof!

**Inchnacardoch** (S.W. of village). Fine forest walk along R. Oich. Picnic site.

See also INVERGARRY, STRATH ERRICK.

**FORTROSE,** Highland     1,000     E.C. Thurs.
10 m. S.W. of Cromarty by A832; 16 m. N.E. of Beauly by A9/A832.

Quiet resort facing Moray Firth. Good centre for exploring Black Isle (not island but broad promontory between Cromarty and Moray Firths). A golf course separates town from Rosenarkie, its twin. Created combined royal burgh in 1592.

**Fortrose Cathedral. D.E.** *Apr. to Sept. 9.30-7 weekdays, 2-7 Sun.; Oct. to Mar. 9.30-4 weekdays, 2-4 Sun.* Dates from 14th c. Founded by David I. Portions of cathedral still complete with some fine detail.

**Rosemarkie** (Chanonry Point). Magnificent views across Moray Firth to Fort George.

**Hugh Miller's Cottage. N.T.S.** Cromarty. 9 m. N.E. of Fortrose by A832. *Apr. to end Oct. 10-12, 2-5 weekdays; also Sun. June to Sept. only 2-5.* Hugh Miller (1802-56) noted geologist, born here. Museum has interesting items akin to Miller's work and life.

**Regattas:** Fortrose and Cromarty, *August.*

See also REDCASTLE, DUNDROCHIT HILL, UDALE BAY.

**FORT WILLIAM,** Highland     4,000     E.C. Wed. (out
                                                    of season)
66 m. S.W. of Inverness by A82; 49 m. N.E. of Oban by A85/A828/A82.

*i* Area Tourist Office. (0397) 3581.

Takes its name from fort built in 1655 by General Monk. One of major touring centres in Scottish Highlands. Traffic delays in the town can be lengthy during the peak summer months. Mighty, much-photographed **Ben Nevis** (4,406 ft.) dominates the surroundings and attracts a great many serious mountaineers and, alas, just as many casual, ill-equipped hill walkers.

**West Highland Museum.** *Mid June/mid Sept. 9.30-1, 2-5 weekdays.* Contains all types of exhibits on Fort William and its environs. Interesting section devoted to tartans.

**Caledonian Canal.** Banavie. 3 m. N.E. at entrance to L. Linnhe. Eight locks raise the canal some 65 ft. Generally known as Neptune's Staircase.

**Commando Memorial.** 11 m. N.E. off A82 at B8004. Commemorates the commandos of World War II, many of whom trained in the surrounding area. The work of Scott Sutherland, it was erected in 1952.

**Glenfinnan Monument. N.T.S.** 18 m. W. by A830 on L. Shielside. Here, in 1745, Prince Charles Edward Stuart (Young Pretender) raised his standard. Monument commemorates historic occasion with inscription in Gaelic, English and Latin.

**'Road to the Isles'.** 26 m. N.E. Refers to A87 from Invergarry to Kyle of Lochalsh. One of the truly fine scenic routes of Britain, it passes the well-known Eilean Donan Castle near Dornie. Be warned, it can be busy in summer!

**Ben Nevis Race.** *Early September.*

**Glenfinnan Highland Gathering.** *August.*

See also GLEN NEVIS, ROY BRIDGE, TULLOCH, KINLOCHEIL, NORTH BALLACHULISH.

**FRASERBURGH,** Grampian      11,000      E.C. Wed.
43 m. N. of Aberdeen by A92; 26 m. E. of Banff by A98.

*i* Saltoun Sq. (034 62) 2315.

Busy fishing port with interesting harbour. Favourite N.E. holiday resort offering good sand beaches. Bracing air — seagulls galore. Rosehearty, 3 m. W. by B9031, is a pretty little village full of character and quiet appeal.

See also SANDHAVEN, PITSLIGO, PENNAN, INVERALLOCHY.

**GAIRLOCH,** Highland   125   E.C. Wed. (out of season).
74 m. N.W. of Inverness by A9/A832; 48 m. S.W. of Ullapool by A835/A832.

*i* Area Tourist Office, Achtercairn (0445) 2130.

Gairloch is within easy reach of some of most spectacular scenery in N.W. Highlands. Lovely L. Maree, an angler's paradise, is nearby and there are some good sign-posted walks. Big Sand (nr. village) is, as name suggests, a lengthy beach. Given good weather the drive to Ullapool via Gruinard Bay and Dundonnell can be memorable. So too are the trips to Achnasheen by A832 and Torridon and Shieldaig by A832/A896.

**Inverewe Gardens.** N.T.S. 6 m. N.E. by A832. *Dawn till dusk, all year. Visitor Centre Apr.-mid Oct. 10-6.30 weekdays, 1-6.30 Sun.* Here, on a latitude further N. than that of Moscow, are famous woodland gardens, semi-tropical plants and the much-photographed palm trees. You'll not be alone — upwards of 100,000 people visit the Gardens each year!

**Beinn Eighe National Nature Reserve.** (nr. Kinlochewe) 19 m. S.E. by A832. Founded in 1951; controlled by Nature Conservancy Council. Visitor Centre. Meet some of Scotland's less common animals and birds . . . the wildcat, mountain goat, golden eagle, etc. Geologically interesting too.

See also BADACHRO, MELVAIG, AULTBEA, MELLON UDRIGLE

**GALASHIELS,** Borders      13,000      E.C. Wed.
33 m. S.E. of Edinburgh by A7; 19 m. E. of Peebles by A72.

*i* St John's Street (0896) 55551.

Well-known for manufacture of textiles. Lies on Gala Water near its confluence with the great R. Tweed. Fine rolling hills surround and make for pleasant distraction from somewhat industrial town. The important Scottish College of Textiles is in Netherdale.

🐾 **Abbotsford House.** 3 m. S.E. by A7. *Late Mar.-end Oct. 10-5 weekdays, 2-5 Sun.* The great novelist Sir Walter Scott (born 1771) spent much of his life here. He died in this House in 1832. Within the grounds are many trees planted by Scott himself. See vast library of about 9,000 volumes and other historical relics. Drawing-room contains many interesting portraits and armoury has fine collection of weapons.

🐾 **Scottish Museum of Wool Textiles.** Walkerburn. 13 m. W. by W A72. *Open throughout year. 9-5 Mon./Fri.; 11-4 Sat.; 2-4 Sun.* Clearly depicts the expansion of the Scottish textile trade. Much of interest including hand spinning demonstrations.

**Galashiels Braw Lads Gathering.** *June.*

See also ASHIESTEEL, INNTERLEITHEN, DARNICK.

**GATEHOUSE OF FLEET,** Dumf. and Gall.                    1,000
                                                          E.C. Thurs.
19 m. S.E. of Newton Stewart by A75; 31 m. S.W. of Dumfries by A75.

*i* Information Centre Car Park (055 74) 212.

Pleasantly situated on Water of Fleet. Colourful little cottages attract the eye as do the green hills W. and N. of town. In what is now a comfortable hotel Burns wrote the well known verses of his 'Scots Wha Hae'.

**Cardonness Castle. D.E.** 1 m. S.W. by A75. *Apr. to Sept. 9.30-7 weekdays, 2-7 Sun. Oct. to Mar. 9.30-4 weekdays, 2-4 Sun.* Dates from 15th c. Formerly home of the McCullochs of Galloway. Feature of well-preserved tower-house is stairway, this being in its original form.

/ **Fleet Forest Trails** (south of town). Excellent walks in an unspoilt environment.

See also ANWOTH CHURCH.

**GIRVAN,** Strathclyde      7,500       E.C. Wed.
22 m. S.W. of Ayr by A77; 30 m. N. of Stranraer by A77.

Bridge St. (0465) 2056/7.

Popular seaside resort with good amenities for young and old. Offshore sea angling can be excellent as can sea-trout fishing in nearby Girvan Water. The fringes of the vast Galloway

Forest Park (see Newton Stewart) are but a dozen miles inland.

**Barr.** 8 m. S.E. by B734. Often regarded as being one of prettiest villages in S.W. Scotland. It is. Good fishing (by permit) in nearby R. Stinchar.

**Ballantrae.** 13 m. S.W. by A77. Coast road via Kennedy's Pass and Lendalfoot offers fine views seawards to Ailsa Craig and Arran. Watch — and **only watch** — the salmon lying in R. Stinchar beneath road bridge (S. end of village).

**Glenapp Castle Gardens.** 15 m. S.W. by A77. *Easter to Sept. 10-5 daily ex. Sat.* Extensive gardens, woodland walks and an air of tranquillity.

**Turnberry.** 5 m. N. by A.77. Small resort facing Ailsa Craig (see previous entry) and the mountains of Arran. Noted for its two golf courses which occasionally stage the British "Open". Splendidly sited and appointed Turnberry Hotel is among Britain's best.

**Ailsa Craig.** 10 m. offshore. Reached by boat hired from Girvan harbour. Peculiarly shaped rock rising steeply from sea, to 1,114 ft. Teems with seabirds. Noted for its granite used in the making of high quality curling stones.

**GLASGOW,** Strathclyde    816,000    E.C. Tues. (suburbs) 45 m. W. of Edinburgh by A8/M8; 26 m. S.W. of Stirling by M80/A80.

George Square. (041) 221 7371/2; (041) 221 6136/7.

**Weather:** (041) 246 8091

Largest populated city in Scotland and third in British Isles after London and Birmingham. The expansion of Glasgow dates from 17th c. when the city's merchants "cashed in" on tobacco, sugar and cotton, then produce of the New World. Much later (19th c.) came a second great boom which made Glasgow a major centre for heavy industry and a forerunner in the building of ships of all sizes from Clyde 'puffers' (coal carrying boats) to the giant Cunarders — Queens Mary, Elizabeth and the present day QE2. Sadly much of this vast industrial power has now gone due largely to Britain's economic decline over the last decade and to fierce competition from world markets. Like all other great centres of population Glasgow has its slums, its drunkenness and more than its fair share of hardened and potentially hardened criminals. On the other side of the coin it has the country's only opera house (Theatre Royal), is the home of the Scottish National Orchestra and has some of the best-kept public parks in Britain. Not leasts, it has an abundance of unrivalled scenery on its very doorstep. Today Glasgow boasts the most successful independent local radio station in Britain — Radio Clyde; an underground railway system (the 'subway') which has been running since 1896 (re-opened *Nov.*, 1979) modernisation) and, in Hampden Park, a soccer stadium which held 149,547 fans at the Scotland v England international on 17th April, 1937. Above all, Glasgow is full of a warm-heartedness that is hard to find in other major cities . . . little wonder it's known as the friendliest city on earth. Visitors will form their own opinion.

🐘 **Glasgow Cathedral.** High St./adjacent Glasgow Royal Infirmary. *Apr. to Sept. 10-7 weekdays, 1-6 Sun,; Oct. to Mar. 10-5.30 weekdays, 1-6 Sun.* Dates from 12th c. Few realise that this is incomparably the finest intact Gothic building in Scotland. Crypt generally regarded as one of the grandest in British Isles.

🐘 **Provand's Lordship.** High St. opp. Glasgow Cathedral. *Apr.*
w *to Sept. 10-5 daily; Oct. to Mar. 10-4 daily.* Glasgow's oldest house c. 1471. Mary, Queen of Scots stayed here in 1566. Interesting 17th c. furniture, stained glass, tapestries and portraits.

🐘 **Art Gallery and Museum.** Kelvingrove Park, opp. Kelvin
w Hall. *All year 10-5 weekdays, 2-5 Sun.* Contains Britain's finest civic art collection, notably Rembrandt's "A Man in Armour". Salvador Dali's "Christ of St. John of the Cross" (1951) attracts considerable attention. Parts of the famous Burrell collection, 8,000 works of art gifted to the city in 1944, are often shown. A point of interest . . . this building is somewhat unique in that its main entrance was designed to face N. towards the University on Gilmorehill with a rear exit to Sauchiehall St. Visitors will find that, in practice, the reverse happens with, in fact, little coming and going at the true front of the building. Nearby is a recently-built
🛹 skateboard rink.

🐘 **Hunterian Museum.** Glasgow University/University Ave. off
w Byres Rd. *All year 9-5 Mon./Fri., 9-12 Sat.* Oldest museum in Glasgow (1807). Archaeological items are noteworthy. See also collection of Chinese jade.

🐘 **People's Palace.** Glasgow Green. S.E. of city centre. *All year*
w *10-5 weekdays, 2-5 Sun.* Specialises in all aspects of Glasgow's development over past 1,000 or so years. Interesting models of Tolbooth, etc.

🐘 **Museum of Transport.** Albert Dr. off Pollokshaws Rd. S. of
🛹 city centre. *All year 10-5 weekdays, 2-5 Sun.* Generally
w regarded as being one of the best of its kind. Horse-drawn

vehicles, fire engines and everything to take the eye of curious little boys and girls.

w **Botanic Gardens.** (at Great Western Rd./Byres Rd. N.W. of city centre). *Summer 7-dusk.* Has all that one might expect to find in a great city's gardens. See also **Kibble Palace** *(open 10-4.45 weekdays, 12-4.45 Sun.)* with its fine collection of rare tree-ferns, etc.

**Calderpark Zoo.** 6 m. S.E. by Gallowgate or London Rd.
w (A74). *All year 9.30-7 (or dusk if earlier) daily.*
One of the country's premier zoos, Calderpark provides a pleasant outing.

**Crookston Castle.** N.T.S./D.E. 4 m. S.W. off Paisley Road West. *Apr. to Sept. 9.30-7 weekdays, 2-7 Sun.; Oct. to Mar. 9.30-4 weekdays, 2-4 Sun.* Early 15th c. ruin. Here Mary, Queen of Scots and Darnley stayed in 1565.

**Haggs Castle.** St. Andrew's Drive, Pollokshields, approx. 1 m. S. Kingston Bridge/M8. *All year 10-6.15 Mon./Sat. 2-5 Sun.* Particularly interesting to children. Museum has emphasis on history with a difference. Here the visitors are invited to take part in various activities including one which lets them experiment in 17th c. cookery recipes.

**Pollok House.** Pollokshaws Rd., 3 m. S.W. city centre. (A736). 18th c. mansion noted for its fine collection of paintings. Some interesting pieces of furniture, pottery, porcelain, etc., are also shown. Pleasant wooded parkland.

**Provan Hall.** N.T.S. 4 m. E. of city centre off A8 Edinburgh Rd. at Stepps. *All year: contact caretaker at (041) 771 1538.* Well restored 15th c. house often regarded as being finest building of its period within Scotland.

**P.S. 'Waverley'.** Last sea-going paddle steamer in the world. Regular cruises and sailings in summer from Stobcross Quay, (N. bank of river near Kingston Bridge) to Clyde coast resorts

such as Dunoon, Rothesay and Largs. For sailing times etc. apply to Waverley S.N. Co. Ltd. Stobcross Quay, Glasgow. Tel. (041) 221 8152.

**City Bus Tours.** Two-hour city sightseeing tours by double-decker bus operate from N. Hanover St. (near George Sq. and G.P.O.) each afternoon. Can be interesting once clear of the concrete jungle of office blocks!

See also (within Glasgow). George Square/City Chambers, Mitchell Library (North St.), Fossil Grove (Victoria Park) and, for architecture, Great Western Road (terraces near Kirklee), St. Vincent St. Church (city centre area) and Glasgow School of Art (Renfrew St. nr. Sauchiehall St.).

**GLENCOE,** Highland   195   E.C. Wed.
36 m. N.W. of Crianlarich by A82; 16 m. S. of Fort William by A82.

*i* Claymore Filling Station (085 52) 296.

**N.T.S. Visitor Centre** (085 52) 307 *mid-May to mid-Oct. 10-6 weekdays, 2-6 Sun.* N.T.S. owns over 14,000 acres of Glencoe and Dalness. Wildlife (deer, ptarmigan, etc.) is notable.

By far the best known of Scotland's many glens. Strictly speaking this famous 'glen of weeping' starts near the boundary separating the Strathclyde and Highland regions and runs W. towards Glencoe village. The mountains here are wild and magnificent. Indeed, it has been said "there are no superlatives too extravagant for this valley" through which runs the A82 trunk road to Fort William and Inverness. Sometimes it can look "like a cold, wet corner of hell". The mean annual rainfall is about 90 inches whereas much of the rest of Scotland has less than 30 inches!

**Glencoe and North Lorn Folk Museum.** Glencoe village. *June to Sept. 10-5 Mon./Sat.* Interesting collection of relics associated with Prince Charles Edward Stuart (Young Pretender) and other items such as dolls and dolls' houses.

**Massacre of Glencoe.** This was centred in the area around the Pap of Glencoe (2,430 ft.) and Glencoe village itself. Site of the massacre where, in 1692, Government troops slew 38 Macdonalds who had been slow in showing their allegiance to William III, is commemorated by a monument in village.

**The Study** (approached from S. 4½ m. past the Glenetive fork bearing left). Most would agree that from here one gets the best view of the Glen. On the S. side of A82 are the well known "Three Sisters of Glencoe" all of which are between 2,500 and 3,000 ft. high.

**White Corries Ski Centre.** 11 m. E. by A82 and unclass. road.

*Normally closed during Mar. Apr. May and Sept.* Chairlitt,
※ ski-tows and wonderful scenery.

See also CARNACH, BALLACHULISH, ONICH (view).

**GRANTOWN-ON-SPEY,** Highland    1,500    E.C. Thurs.
15 m. N.E. of Aviemore by A9/A95; 35 m. S.E. of Inverness
by A9/A938.

*(* The Square (0479) 2773.

Delightful all-year resort in Strath Spey. Ski-ing and après-ski
facilities are excellent as is fishing in Spey, one of Scotland's
major rivers. Cairngorm mountains are within easy reach.

**Lochindorb Castle.** 10 m. N.W. by A939 and unclass. road.
Dates from 13th c. Ruined castle (on island) formerly
belonged to Comyns and for time was occupied by Edward
※ III. Splendid views looking W. from the bleak Dava Moor
can be enjoyed.

**Nethybridge.** 4 m. S. by B970 has a Highland Gathering in
August.

See also DULNAIN BRIDGE, TOMINTOUL (highest village
in Highlands).

**GRETNA GREEN,** Dumf. and Gall.    2,000 (with Gretna)
E.C. Wed.
8 m. E. of Annan by A.75; 1 m. N.W. of English border by
A.74.

*(* Annan Road (Gretna) (046 13) 834.

Much visited "Gateway to Scotland", Gretna Green and its
environs have long been associated with romance and history
in the form of clandestine marriages which took place here
up until 1940.

🐦 **Old Blacksmith's Shop.** Situated on A.6071 at top of village.
This old clay daubin made Gretna Green famous. Thousands
of marriages took place in front of the now famous anvil.
Conducted tours of premises cater for world-wide visitors.
Interesting curios. Gifts and souvenirs.

🐦 **Toll Inn (Sark Bridge).** Lies virtually on Scotland/England
border here formed by sluggish R. Sark. 1 m. S.E. of Gretna
Green by A74. Brisk business in Scottish gifts and souvenirs,
the toll-house bears witness to no fewer than 10,000
runaway marriages within the space of a few years. Rightly
bears the tag "First House in Scotland".

**Lochmaben Stone.** 1 m. S. via Old Gretna and minor road.
This 7 ft. high stone, said to weigh over 10 tons, was once
part of a stone circle and is a known meeting-place between

the Scots and English who gathered here in 1398 to discuss a possible truce.

**HADDINGTON,** Lothian    7,000    E.C. Thurs.
17 m. E. of Edinburgh by A1/slip road; 12 m. S.W. of Dunbar by A1/slip road and A1087.
Pleasant 18th c. town on R. Tyne. There are some delightful little villages nearby, notably Pencaitland, Gifford and Athelstaneford.

**Town House** (town centre). Dates from 1748. The work of William Adam it is extremely well proportioned. There are several dignified 17th-19th c. streets nearby.

**St. Mary's Pleasance** (outskirts of town). *Open all reasonable times.* Delightful gardens of Haddington House.

**Hailes Castle. D.E.** 5 m. E. off A1. *Apr. to Sept. 9.30-7 weekdays, 2-7 Sun; Oct to Mar. 9.30-4 weekdays, 2-4 Sun.* Extensive ruins dating from 13th to 15th c. Dismantled by Cromwell in 1650. It retains the original water-gate and dungeons.

**Gifford Church.** 5 m. S.E. by B6369. *All reasonable times.* Dates from 1708. Interesting late medieval bell and 17th c. pulpit.

**Winton House.** 6 m. S.W. by A1/B6355. Enquiries re. viewing Tel. (0875) 340222. Dates from 1620 though with 19th c. additions. A masterpiece of Scottish Renaissance architecture. See chimney stacks, plaster ceilings, pictures and furniture.

**Museum of Flight.** 5 m. N.E. by A1/B1347 at East Fortune airfield. *June/Jul. 10-4 daily.* Varied collection of aircraft are shown from old gyroplanes to modern jets.

**Myreton Motor Museum.** 5 m. N. by A6137/B1377. *Easter to Oct. 10-6 daily. Oct. to Mar. weekends only.* Good collection of cars, commercial vehicles, motor cycles, etc. Children will be enthralled.

**Aberlady Church.** 5 m. N.W. by A6137. *All reasonable times.* Tower dates from 15th c. Fine stained-glass windows are notable.

See also BOLTON, GARVALD.

**HAMILTON,** Strathclyde,    45,000    E.C. Wed.
10 m. S.E. of Glasgow by A724; 15 m. N.W. of Lanark by A72.

*ℓ* Galleon Roadchef M74, via slip road (42) 59124.

A pleasant town made more attractive since it was by-passed

# Visit the
# DAVID LIVINGSTONE CENTRE

Memorial to the Great Scottish
Missionary Explorer

AFRICAN PAVILION, SHUTTLE ROW
MUSEUM. MODERN TEA ROOM AND
SHOP, PLAY AREA FOR CHILDREN,
PADDLING POOL.
LARGE CAR PARK.

*OPEN DAILY 10am till 6pm.*
*SUNDAY 2pm till 6pm.*

ALL AT BLANTYRE, LANARKSHIRE
8 MILES FROM GLASGOW.

by the busy M74 Glasgow-Carlisle road. The surroundings tend to be industrial with poorish scenery but there are many points of interest within easy reach. Hamilton racecourse holds regular meetings.

🐾 **Hamilton Mausoleum** (outskirts of town). Enquiries re. viewing Tel. (42) 24940. Built about 1850 by 10th Duke of Hamilton. It is well-known for its remarkable echo. See also bronze doors inside building.

🐾 **David Livingstone National Memorial.** Blantyre. 3 m. N.W.
w by A724. *Open all year 10-6 weekdays, 2-6 Sun.* The famous explorer/missionary was born here (Shuttle Row) in 1813. Museum contains many interesting relics of his career and gives one an impression of life during the Industrial Revolution. **See ad on facing page.**

w **Bothwell Castle. D.E.** 2½ m. N.W. by A74. *Apr. to Sept. 9.30-7 weekdays, 2-7 Sun.; Oct. to Mar. 9.30-4 weekdays, 2-4 Sun.* Built 13th c. by family of de Moravia. Reconstructed by Douglases in 15th c. Now an extensive ruin, with walls upwards of 15 ft. thick in parts. Possibly the finest 13th c. castle in Scotland. Nearby is Bothwell Brig where, in a fierce battle (1679), the Covenanters were defeated by the Duke of Monmouth and Graham of Claverhouse.

🐾🐾 **Strathclyde Regional Park.** (1,600 acres lying between Hamilton and Motherwell). Work on this vast project started in 1973. Varied amenities include a boating lake, golf course, children's play area and, for ornithologists, a heronry. Much more is planned though a recent survey, disturbing to rate-payers, has shown that some 80% of all those using the park are, in fact, walking their dog!

See also CATHKIN BRAES (view), STRATHAVEN, ROSE-BANK.


**HAWICK,** Borders      16,000      E.C. Tues.
14 m. S.W. of Jedburgh by A698/B6358; 12 m. S. of Selkirk by A7.

*ℓ* Volunteer Park (0450) 2547.

Largest of the Border towns it is noted as a woollen-manufac-turing centre of world repute. Good fishing in R. Teviot. The Yarrow and Ettrick Waters, some dozen miles north of Hawick, offer delightful river settings amid possibly the finest scenery in south Scotland.

🐾 **Hawick Museum and Art Gallery** (Wilton Lodge Park). *Apr.*
w *to Oct. 10-5 Mon./Sat. 2-5 Sun.; Nov. to Mar. 10-4 Mon./ Sat.* Splendid collection of relics akin to Scottish Borders,

Hawick and environs. A section deals in some detail with the history of the woollen trade.

**Hermitage Castle. D.E.** 12 m. S. by B6399. *Apr. to Sept. 9.30-7 weekdays, 2-7 Sun.; Oct. to Mar. 9.30-4 weekdays, 2-4 Sun.* Founded 13th c. One of largest and best preserved in the Borders. Earl of Bothwell (Mary, Queen of Scots lover) owned this castle and Mary visited him (1566) when he was ill. In excellent condition are the building's four towers and connecting walls.

**Hawick Common Riding.** Possibly the best of all the Border Common Riding Festivals. Held early *June* and lasts for two days *(Fri. and Sat.).* Celebrates a victory by the local 'callants' (youths) who, in 1514, defeated an English force at Hornshole Bridge, 2½ m. distant. The Horse Monument (High St.) also recalls the event.

See also BONCHESTER BRIDGE, DENHOLM, HASSEN-DEAN, ROBERTON.

**HELENSBURGH,** Strathclyde   14,000 E.C. Wed.
23 m. N.W. of Glasgow by A.82/A.814; 17 m. S. of Arrochar by A.814.

*i* Pier Head Car Park (0436) 2642.

Fairly modern town near mouth of Gareloch with good views across Clyde estuary. Sailing, good hotels, shops and attractions for all ages. Cruises and sailings on P.S. Waverley. J. Logie Baird, pioneer of TV, was born here in 1888.

**Henry Bell Obelisk.** Memorial to designer of one of earliest steamboats, "Comet", 1812.

**Hill House.** Built 1902 by Charles Rennie Mackintosh, famous Glasgow architect. Examples of Mackintosh furniture, etc. *Tues., Thur., Fri., 1-8; Wed., Sun., 9-5; Sat., 12-5.*

**Glenarm Gardens** (Rhu) 2 m. N.W. by A.814. Rhododendrons, azaleas, magnolias making a blaze of colour. *Mar.-Aug., daily, 9-9.*

See also WHISTLEFIELD, ROSENEATH, GLEN FRUIN.

**HUNTLY,** Grampian   4,000   E.C. Thurs.
39 m. N.W. of Aberdeen by A96; 21 m. S.W. of Banff by A97.

*i* The Square (0466) 2255.

Attractive town at confluence of rivers Bogie and Deveron. Seat of once-powerful Gordon family, one of whom bore the

75

title 'Cock o' the North'. Good angling especially in nearby Deveron.

**Huntly Castle. D.E.** *Apr. to Sept. 9.30-7 weekdays, 2-7 Sun.;* w *Oct. to Mar. 9.30-4 weekdays, 2-4 Sun.* A 15th c. ruin, one of noblest in Scotland. The topmost storey has original elaboration of early 17th c. period.

**Leith Hall. N.T.S.** 7 m. S. by A97/B9002. *May to Sept. 11-1, 2-6 weekdays, 2-6 Sun.* An attractive old country house dating from 1650. Fine collection of family treasures notably of a military nature. The Trust also has charge of the beautiful gardens *(open all year from 10-dusk).*

See also KEITH, DUFFTOWN, RHYNIE.

**INVERARAY,** Strathclyde   500   E.C. Wed. (out of season) 59 m. N.W. of Glasgow by A82/A83; 38 m. S.E. of Oban by A85/A819.

*i* Information Centre (0499) 2063.

An attractive little place on L. Fyne. Thronged with tourists during the summer — and other times too! Much of the filming for the T.V. series 'Vital Spark' was shot hereabouts. Good fishing in loch and local rivers (permit).

**Inveraray Castle.**
        Home of the Dukes of Argyll and headquarters of Clan Campbell since early 15th c. Impressive building with its well kept lawns sloping gently to nearby R. Aray. A serious fire (1975) partly destroyed the castle and some treasures but fund-raising has brought about considerable restoration. Fine family portraits by Gainsborough, Ramsay and Raeburn. Great Hall, armoury, state rooms. Gift shop and tea room. Pleasant woodland walks to summit of hill, Dun na Cuaiche. *April to Jun 30, 10-12.30, 2-6, daily ex. Fri. July to early Oct. 10-6 daily. Suns., 2-6.*

**Castle Fisheries.** 3 m. up Glen Aray. Interesting trout farm with hatcheries. Trout fishing available.

**Glen Aray.** (A819). A delightful glen by any standard. Excellent views from 1-2 m. up Glen and again on descent to Cladich (9 m.) From here it is worth deviating by B840 to Portsonachan on Loch Aweside . . . again for the fine view.

**Auchindrain Museum.** 6 m. S.W. by A83. *Easter to end Sept.,weekdays 10-6;Sun.,2-6.* Depicts rural life and farming habits akin to this part of Scotland.     Past rather than present is emphasised in the exhibits. **See ad. at back.**

**Crarae Gardens.** 10 m. S.W. by A83. *Mar. to Oct. 8-6 daily.* Considered by some to be the loveliest gardens open to the

public in Scotland. Delightfully set on L. Fyneside. Rhododendrons, azaleas and conifers are noteworthy.

**Strone Gardens.** 10 m. E. by A83/A815. *Mar. to Sept. 9-7
daily.* Daffodils, primulas, exotic shrubs and much, much
more. Here too is the tallest tree in Britain, a 188 ft. high fir
(abies grandis).

**Inveraray Highland Games.** *July.*

See also GLEN SHIRA (Rob Roy's House), GLEN FYNE.
ST. CATHERINES, LOCHGOILHEAD (via Hell's Glen).

**INVERNESS,** Highland    36,500    E.C. Wed.
66 m. N.E. of Fort William by A82; 38 m. W. of Elgin by
A96.

*i* 23 Church St. (0463) 34353.

Capital of the Highlands lying astride R. Ness, here six miles
downstream from the monster-famed Loch. Important
touring centre for Moray coast and Black Isle. Inverness was
on map of Scotland in AD 565 when St. Columba visited a
nearby castle. About this time it was capital of the Pictish
kingdom. Much later (c. 1652) Cromwell erected a fort, of
which now only a clock tower remains. Today the inhabitants
of this busy resort have in their speech probably the truest
form of spoken English — and this in a town which is headquarters of the Gaelic language and culture! Anglers should
note that Inverness is somewhat unique. It is the only large
place in Britain where one can fish for salmon (and catch
them) virtually from its town centre.

**Inverness Museum and Art Gallery.** *All year 9-5 Mon./Sat.*
W Emphasis here on everything Highland — costumes,
weapons, folk life, etc. Interesting section on the history of
the clans.

**Culloden Moor. N.T.S.** Visitor Centre. 5 m. E. by B9006. A
cairn marks the site of the famous battle (1746) where Prince
Charles Edward was defeated by the Duke of Cumberland.
Of special interest are the Graves of the Clans and Well of the
Dead. Well worth visiting nearby are the Stones of Clava
(D.E.) dating from the Bronze Age.

**Fort George. D.E.** 11 m. N.E. by A96/B9006. *Apr. to Sept.*
W *9.30-7 weekdays, 2-7 Sun.; Oct. to Mar. 9.30-4 weekdays, 2-4
Sun.* Dates from 18th c. following the 1745 Jacobite rising.
Interesting military museum. Unusual pulpit within chapel.

See also (in Inverness), ABERTARFF HOUSE, HIGH
CHURCH, MERCAT CROSS, ST. ANDREW'S CATH-
EDRAL (Outwith Inverness), CRAIG PHADRIG FOREST
TRAIL (2 m. W. of town centre).

**INVERURIE,** Grampian    5,500    E.C. Wed.
17 m. N.W. of Aberdeen by A96; 23 m. S.E. of Huntly by
A96.

Pleasant little down set in rich agricultural surroundings.
Here R. Don joins forces with Urie and flows S.E. to
Aberdeen. Bennachie, a wooded ridge of about 1,700 ft., is a
local landmark offering good walks over a wide area.

**Pitcaple Castle.** 5 m. N.W. by A96. *May to Sept. 11-6 daily.*
Attractive building with twin towers. Dates from 15th c.
Marquis of Montrose held prisoner here (1650). Museum. 1
m. W. (S. of A96) is the interesting Maiden Stone. See Celtic
Cross and Pictish symbols.

**Castle Fraser. N.T.S.** 8 m. S.W. by B993/unclass. road. *Mid
Mar. to end Apr. and first fortnight Oct. 11-1, 2-6 Wed. also
2-6 Sat. and Sun. May to Sept. 11-6 weekdays, 2-6 Sun.* Dates
from 1575. Six-storeyed Z-plan building. Possibly best
example in Scotland of Flemish-style architecture. Entrance
fee includes Exhibition.

See also THE BASS (B993), KINKELL CHURCH,
KINTORE (Tolbooth and Church).


**ISLAY,** Strathclyde    4,000    E.C. (varies)
Ferries from Kennacraig (Kintyre) to Port Ellen and Port
Askaig. (2-3 hrs. respectively).

*i* Main St. Bowmore (049 681) 254.

Southernmost island of Inner Hebrides. Measures approx.
25 m. by 19 m. Excellent sand beaches are a feature of this
popular isle as is its bird life. Whisky distilling is of major
importance to the community.

**Bowmore Round Church.** *Open all reasonable times.* Dates
from 1769. Now parish church. Circular shape designed so
that no evil spirits could hide within! So the story goes.

**Kildalton Cross.** 7 m. N.E. of Port Ellen by A846/unclass.
road. *All reasonable times.* Apart from that at Iona (see Mull
and Iona), this is probably the finest Celtic cross in Scotland.
Dates from c. 800.

**Museum of Islay Life.** Port Charlotte 11 m. S.W. of
Bowmore by A846/A847. *May to Oct. 10-5 Mon./Fri. 2-5
Sun.; Nov. to Apr. 10-12.30, 1.30-5 Mon./Fri.* Well displayed
exhibits include many domestic items and — an illicit still!
✳ The pretty village with its Gaelic street names offers fine views
of L. Indaal. Attractive restaurant/tea room near shore.

✳ **Rhinns Lighthouse.** Portnahaven/Port Wemyss. 7 m. S.W.
of Port Charlotte by A.847. Slightly offshore on little Orsay
island. Trips by motor boat (5 min. crossing) can be arranged

by contacting the Principal Lightkeeper (Tel: 0496 86 223).

**Portnahaven.** Attractive little village with fine seascapes. Linger awhile and sample some of the country's best tweeds, woollens etc., in local gift shop, **Rocmar** by name. High class souvenirs also available. Accommodation. Tel: 0496 86 236. *Daily.*

**Islay, Jura and Colonsay Agricultural Show.** *August.*

See also MULL OF OA, BRIDGEND, PORT ASKAIG.


**JEDBURGH,** Borders    4,000    E.C. Thurs.

14 m. N.E. of Hawick by A698; 11 m. S.W. of Kelso by A698.

*i* Murray's Green (083 56) 3435.

Formerly county town of Roxburghshire. Thoroughly Scottish yet only 14 m. from the border at Carter Bar.

**Jedburgh Abbey. D.E.** *Apr. to Sept. 9.30-7 weekdays, 2-7 Sun. Oct. to Mar. 9.30-4 weekdays, 2-4 Sun.* Dates from c 1118, now extensive ruins. Founded by David I for French monks. St. Catherine's Wheel (a rose window) and an elaborately carved Norman doorway attract most attention.

**Mary, Queen of Scots House.** *Apr. to Sept. 10-12, 1-5, 6-8 weekdays; 1-5, 6-8 Sun.* Mary, Queen of Scots stayed here (1566). Museum contains many interesting relics akin to Queen, not least her death mask.

**Jail Museum.** *All year 10-12, 1-5 weekdays; 1-5 Sun.* Clearly illustrates the 'reformed' penal system of early 19th c. Museum formerly a prison on site of still earlier Jedburgh Castle.

**Jedburgh Border Games.** *July.*

See also ANCRUM, DENHOLM.


**JOHN O'GROATS,** Highland    200.

142 m. N.E. of Inverness by A9; 20 m. E. of Thurso by A836.

The Scottish equivalent of Land's End, though not quite . . . Scotland's most northerly mainland point is actually 14 m. W. at Dunnet Head. John o'Groats and Duncansby Head (E.) offer fine views of South Ronaldsay and Hoy (Orkneys). Canisbay, 2 m. W. by A836, has the most northerly church in mainland Britain. Here is buried John de Groot, after whose house John o'Groats was named. Castle of Mey, home of Qùeen Elizabeth the Queen Mother, is 2 m. further west.

See also FRESWICK, HUNA.

**JURA,** Strathclyde    200.
Reached by car ferry from Islay (Port Askaig) to Feolin. 5 min. crossing.

Known as 'deer island', and rightly so too . . . there were more than 5,000 at the last estimate. A peaceful place with three conspicuous mountains, the 'Paps'. Fuchsia abound in
🛉🛉 Craighouse, the main village. Boat trips arranged to famous whirlpool of Corryvreckan off N. tip of this totally unspoilt island. Near here George Orwell wrote his well-known '1984'.

**KELSO,** Borders    5,000    E.C. Wed.
11 m. N.E. of Jedburgh by A68/A698; 23 m. S.W. of Berwick-upon-Tweed by A698.

*i* Turret House (057 32) 3464.

Extremely attractive Border town with splendid five-arched bridge spanning majestic R. Tweed near its confluence with Teviot. Wide, cobbled market square, lanes and appealing houses.

w **Kelso Abbey. D.E.** *Apr. to Sept. 9.30-7 weekdays, 2-7 Sun.; Oct. to Mar. 9.30-4 weekdays, 2-4 Sun.* Founded by David I (1128). Destroyed by Earl of Hertford's English army in 1545. Tower and parts of the nave are virtually all now remaining.

🐿 **Floors Castle.** 2 m. N.W. off A6089. *Early May to late Sept. 1.30-5.30 daily ex. Fri. and Sat.* Vast mansion built by Wm. Adam in 1721. Home of Roxburghe family. Tapestries, furniture, porcelain, paintings and fine gardens. Splendid
❋ views of nearby R. Tweed. Restaurant and gift shop.

🐿 **Smailholm Tower. D.E.** 7 m. W. off B6404. *Apr. to Sept.*
w *9.30-7 weekdays, 2-7 Sun.; Oct. to Mar. 9.30-4 weekdays, 2-4 Sun.* Well preserved Border tower of 16th c. (Note: Key normally held at adjoining farmhouse.)

🐿 **Mellerstain House.** 8 m. N.W. by A6089/unclass. road. *May to end Sept. 1.30-5.30 daily ex. Sat.* Built by the Adams (William and Robert) between 1725 and 1765. Probably Scotland's most famous Adam house. Magnificent ceilings, antique furniture and paintings. Outstanding views of
❋ Cheviot Hills, etc. from garden terrace.

**Borders Fair.** Kelso and other Border towns. Two weeks *(late May-early June).*

See also EDNAM, YETHOLM, ROXBURGH.

**KILLIN,** Central    500    E.C. Wed.
44 m. W. of Perth by A85/A827; 23 m. S.W. of Aberfeldy by A827.

# FLOORS CASTLE

## KELSO

**Home of the Duke and Duchess of Roxburghe**

Situated in the beautiful and historic Border country
and overlooking the River Tweed, the town of Kelso,
and the ruins of Roxburgh Castle, Floors Castle is
open to the public from early May to late September.

The Castle, built in 1721 by William Adam and later
added to by Playfair, is still used today as it was
conceived — as the home of the Roxburghe family.

Open daily (except Fridays and Saturdays) from 4th
May to 25th September 1980. Grounds and gardens
12.30 — 5.30 p.m. House 1.30 p.m. (last admission
4.45 p.m.) Garden Centre, Restaurant and Gift Shop.

Party Rates on request. All enquiries to:
The Factor, Roxburghe Estates Office, Kelso.
Tel. Kelso 3333

*i* Main St. (056 72) 254.

Possibly one of most photographed villages in Scotland on account of its eye-catching Falls of Dochart. A delightful place in summer (many amenities) and winter (ski-ing on slopes of Ben Lawers.) Good fishing on nearby L. Tay.

**Finlarig Castle D.E.** ½ m. N. *All reasonable times.* Dates from 17th c. Now a neglected ruin. Formerly seat of Breadalbane family. Beheading pit is possibly last surviving example in Scotland.

**Ben Lawers Visitor Centre. N.T.S.** 8 m. N.W. by A827/unclass. road. *May to Sept. 10-5.30 daily.* 1,400 ft. up the great Ben. Tells you all you want to know about the 3,984 ft. high mountain and its Alpine flora which grows here as in no other part of Britain. Guided walks arranged.

**Lochearnhead.** 8 m. S. by A827/A85. Picturesquely set village at westernmost tip of 7 m. long loch. Fine scenery but above all famous as a centre for aquatic sports, especially water ski-ing.

**Lix Toll.** 2 m. S. Name given to junction where A827 meets with A85. So called on account of its being 59 road miles from Edinburgh.

**Lochearnhead Highland Games.** *July.*

See also FALLS OF LOCHAY, ST. FILLANS, KENMORE.

**KINGUSSIE,** Highland      1,000      E.C. Wed.
45 m. N.W. of Pitlochry by A9; 45 m. S. of Inverness by A9.
*i* High St. (054 02) 297.

The village, with nearby Newtonmore, is well organised for both summer and winter holidays. Area has long been associated with pony trekking. Much magnificent scenery with profusion of lofty peaks.

**Highland Folk Museum (Am Fasgadh).** *May to Sept. 10-4 weekdays.* Interesting collection of objects akin to Highland life and customs, both past and present (mainly the former).

**Ruthven Barracks. D.E.** *All reasonable times.* Ruins dating from 1716. A reminder of the '45 uprising. General Wade made alterations but Highlanders destroyed all in 1746.

**Clan Macpherson Museum.** Newtonmore. 3 m. S.W. by A9. *Easter to Sept. 10-1, 2-6 weekdays.* Relics of Prince Charles Edward Stuart.

**Newtonmore Highland Games.** *August.*

See also FESHIE BRIDGE, GARVAMORE BRIDGE — GENERAL WADE'S ROAD — CORRIEYAIRACK PASS.

**KINROSS,** Tayside      3,000      E.C. Thurs.
21 m. N.E. of Stirling by A91/slip road; 30 m. S.W. of St.
Andrews by A91.

Well known angling resort. Nearby L. Leven has long been
famous for its good returns of heavy trout. The attractive
Lomond Hills lie a little way off to the E.

🐾 **Loch Leven Castle. D.E.** (on Castle Island, L. Leven, reached
by ferry). *May to early Oct. 10-6 weekdays; 2-6 Sun.* Tower,
in which Mary, Queen of Scots, was imprisoned for nearly a
year dates from early 14th c. It was from here, in 1568, that
the Queen made her celebrated escape having first been ably
assisted by the gaoler's son!

🐾 **Castle Campbell. D.E.** Dollar. 11 m. W. by A91. *Apr. to*
W *Sept. 9.30-7 weekdays; 2-7 Sun.; Oct. to Mar. 9.30-4 weekdays, 2-4 Sun.* Late 15th c. Formerly known as Castle Gloom.
Stronghold of the Argylls. Worth seeing is the old hall and
fine stone roof.

**Kinross Agricultural Show.** *August.*

**Kinross Festival of Traditional Music and Song.** *Sept.*

See also VANE FARM NATURE RESERVE, GLEN FARG,
GLEN DEVON.


**KIRKCUDBRIGHT,** Dumf. and Gall.      2,500      E.C. Thurs.
28 m. S.W. of Dumfries by A75/A711; 52 m. E. of Stranraer
by A75/A755.

𝓵 Harbour Square (0557) 30494.

One of most ancient towns in Scotland. Popular with artists,
it is probably the most attractive little place on the entire
Solway. The name Kirkcudbright is, in fact, pronounced Kir-
coo-bry.

🐾 **Broughton House.** *Open 11-1, 2-4 Mon./Fri.* Dates from 18th
W c. A fine mansion and an equally fine garden. Former
property of E. A. Hornel the artist.

W **MacLellan's Castle. D.E.** (near Broughton House). *Apr. to
Sept. 9.30-7 weekdays, 2-4 Sun.; Oct. to Mar. 9.30-4 weekdays, 2-4 Sun.* Built in 1582; a ruin since 1752. Prominent
feature in the town and one worth seeing.

🐾 **Stewartry Museum.** *Easter to Oct. 10-12, 1-5 Mon./Sat.*
Depicts the life and work of Kircudbright and its environs.

W **Dundrennan Abbey. D.E.** 7 m. S.E. by A711. *Apr. to Sept.
9.30-7 weekdays, 2-4 Sun.; Oct. to Mar. 9.30-4 weekdays, 2-4
Sun.* Story goes that here Mary, Queen of Scots spent her last
night in Scotland (15th May, 1568). It is said that from Port

Mary, 1½ m. S. of Abbey, she sailed to England. The Cistercian Abbey (1142) is now ruined though the later Chapter House arouses interest.

**Kircudbright Summer Festival.** *July.*

See also (within town) MERCAT CROSS, TOLBOOTH, GREYFRIARS CHURCH (outwith town) BORGUE (B727).

**KYLE OF LOCHALSH,** Highland    500    E.C. Wed.
80 m. W. of Inverness by A9/A832/A890/A87; 75 m. N.W. of Fort William by A82/A87.

*i* Information Centre (0599) 4276.

Gateway to misty Isle of Skye and ideal base for touring Glen Shiel, Lochcarron and Applecross peninsula. Rail terminal of Inverness-Kyle line, one of most scenic routes in Britain. Frequent ferry service to Skye (Kyleakin).

**Eilean Donan Castle.** 9 m. E. off A87. *Easter to Sept. 10-12.30, 2-6 weekdays.* Dates from 1220. Stronghold of the Clan MacRae one of whom is present owner. A picturesquely-set castle now restored, it is connected to the shore by a causeway. At far end of Loch Duich are the impressive range of mountains known as 'Five Sisters of Kintail'.

**Plockton.** 5 m. N. by unclass. road. One of prettiest little seaside villages in Scotland. Flowers, palm trees and yachts predominate . . . little wonder it's an artists' paradise.

**Applecross.** Tiny community whose Gaelic meaning is 'sanctuary' from an original monastry here. Easily reached by ferry to Toscaig, thence road (5 m.) to village. Particularly fine views of Skye and Raasay. Alternatively, the village can be reached by A87/A890/A896 to Kishorn (oil-rig construction) near to which an unclass. road bears W. via the spectacular Pass of the Cattle. A word of warning: the scenery is magnificent, the road isn't!

**Plockton Annual Regatta.** *July.*

See also GLENELG, FALLS OF GLOMACH, STROME CASTLE.

**LAIRG,** Highland    500    E.C. Wed.
59 m. N. of Inverness by A9/A836; 22 m. N.W. of Dornoch by A839/A9/B9168.

*i* Information Centre (0549) 2160.

Noted angling centre on R. and L. Shin. From here, roads radiate to the wilds of W. and N.W. Sutherland, often regarded as being the oldest part of the earth's crust. Nearby is one of the largest hydro-electric schemes in the country.

**Falls of Shin.** 6 m. S. by A836. Much-photographed rocky gorge where salmon leap.

**Gledfield Mill.** 13 m. S. by A836/unclass. road. *June/Aug. 2-6 weekdays.* Built about 1850. A two-storeyed mill formerly used for grinding oatmeal. North is Carbisdale Castle, now one of the largest Youth Hostels in Scotland.

**Bonar Bridge.** 11 m. S. by A836. Three fine forest walks (Kyle of Sutherland) averaging about 2 m.

See also ROSEHALL (Strath Oykel), STRATH CASSLEY, OVERSCAIG (L. Shin), ROGART (Rovie Lodge Gardens).

**LANARK,** Strathclyde      9,000      E.C. Thurs.
25 m. S.E. of Glasgow by A72; 30 m. W. of Peebles by A72.

*i* Information Centre (0555) 4875.

Pleasant town on fringe of Clyde fruit-growing belt. History goes back to 10th c. though nowadays few visible traces of its ancient past are retained. Has important livestock market and, until recently, a racecourse.

**Craignethan Castle. D.E.** 6 m. N.W. off A72. *Apr. to Sept.*
W *9.30-7 weekdays, 2-7 Sun.; Oct. to Mar. 9.30-4 weekdays, 2-4 Sun.* Well-preserved ruin dating from 16th c. Former stronghold of Hamiltons, trustworthy followers of Mary, Queen of Scots.

**New Lanark.** 1 m. S. Visited on account of its picturesque waterfalls on nearby R.Clyde. Corra Linn, a 90 ft. 'fall' is considered the most spectacular. **Corehouse Nature Reserve** is slightly further south.

**St. Bride's Church.** Douglas. 12 m. S.W. by A70. *Apr. to Sept. 9.30-7 weekdays, 2-7 Sun.; Oct. to Mar. 9.30-4 weekdays, 2-4 Sun.* Some interesting tombs are contained in chancel, notably Earl of Angus, died 1514, nicknamed Archibald 'Bell-the-Cat'.

**Gladstone Court Street Museum.** Biggar 13 m. S.E. by A72. *Easter to Oct. 10-12.30, 2-5 Mon./Sat. (note Wed. opening 10-12.30 only).* A delight for all boys and girls. Yes, and adults too! Re-creation of a 19th c. street complete with shops, shopkeepers, school, bank, etc.

**Tinto Hill.** 7 m. S.E. (best approached from Thankerton, A72). A noted viewpoint of S. Scotland. The 2335 ft. hill is considered an easy climb. In good visibility view extends as far S. as Lake District and W. to the N. Ireland coastline.

**Lanark Lanimer Day.** *June.*

See also CROSSFORD, CARLUKE, CARNWATH, SKIRLING (Biggar).

**LARGS,** Strathclyde    9,500    E.C. Wed.
32 m. W. of Glasgow by A737/A760; 14 m. S.W. of Greenock by A742/A78.

*i* Pierhead (0475) 673765.

Much visited Clyde coast holiday resort with good amenities for young and old. The long prom (poorish beach) offers splendid views of the offshore islands, notably Great Cumbrae and Bute. Better still (for the view) is Douglas Park, slightly inland of the seafront. Beyond the S. end of the esplanade a well known local landmark 'the Pencil' commemorates the Battle of Largs (1263).

**Skelmorlie Aisle. D.E.** *Apr. to Sept. 9.30-7 weekdays, 2-7 Sun.* Formerly a church, now a mausoleum with many interesting tombs including that of the founder, Sir Robert Montgomery. Dates from 1636.

**Kelburn Country Centre.** 2 m. S. on A.78. Home of Earls of Glasgow since 1703, Kelburn Castle (not open to public) has glorious views of Firth of Clyde. Country Centre has many attractions — waterfalls, nature walks, garden, pony trekking, adventure course, picnic areas. Shop and exhibitions, snack lunches. Home baking. *May-Sept., daily, 10-6.*

**Cloch Lighthouse.** 11 m. N. by A78. A notable landmark for vessels coming and going on the busy Clyde shipping lanes. The views seawards are magnificent especially that W. to the Cowal peninsula.

**Cornalees Bridge Trail.** 10 m. N.W. by unclass. road. Delightfully quiet spot set high in the hills above Inverkip. Excellent walks. Part of Clyde-Muirshiel Regional Park (see Paisley).

**Magnum Sports Centre,** Irvine. 17 m. S.E. by A78. Possibly the finest indoor sports centre in Scotland. It has just about everything.

**Largs and Millport Regatta.** *July.*

See also WEST KILBRIDE, SEAMILL.

**LEWIS AND HARRIS,** Western Isles    22,000    E.C. (varies) Lewis: reached by car ferry Ullapool (q.v.) to Stornoway (3 hrs.) Harris: car ferry services from Uig (Skye) to Tarbert (2 hrs.)

*i* Lewis (Stornoway) South Beach Quay (0851) 3088

*i* Harris (Tarbert) Information Centre (0859) 2011

Not two islands as is sometimes thought. Oddly they belonged to different counties before regionalisation in 1975. Lewis is a land of great expanses of peat moors, hill lochs large and small and many magnificent sand beaches. Stornoway (pop. 5,000) is a busy fishing port and administrative centre for Western Isles region.

**Lewis:**

**Callanish Standing Stones. D.E.** 15 m. W. of Stornoway, near A858. *Seen all times.* Stonehenge apart, these form the most complete prehistoric site in Britain. A circle of 13 stones (40 ft. diameter) forms most notable part of site. Date: c. 2000 B.C.

**Dun Carloway Broch. D.E.** 15 m. N.W. of Stornoway by A858/ unclass. road. *Apr. to Sept. 9.30-7 weekdays, 2-7 Sun.; Oct. to Mar. 9.30-4 weekdays, 2-4 Sun.* Best example in Hebrides of 'Pictish tower'. Intricate interior is noteworthy. Dates from early Iron Age.

**Shawbost Museum.** 19 m. N.W. of Stornoway by A857/ A858. *Open 10-6 weekdays.* Depicts Lewis's past lifestyle. Interesting Norse mill. See, 5 m. N.E. at Arnol, the Black House — a well preserved example of crofters dwellings in olden times.

See also BUTT OF LEWIS (Port of Ness), EYE PENINSULA

**Harris:**

Famed above all for its tweed, dyed and handwoven here for world markets. Tarbert is principal village. Glorious sand beaches (notably at Luskentyre) are feature of S.W. coastline.

**St. Clement's Church D.E.** Rodel. 23 m. S.W. of Tarbert by A859. *All reasonable times.* Dates from c. 1500. Unusual carvings on tower/gravestones.

**Amhuinnsuid Castle.** 16 m. N.W. by A859/B887. *(No adm.)*

Interesting in that here Sir James Barrie wrote much of his well known 'Mary Rose'.

See also SCALPAY, HUSINISH BAY.

**LINLITHGOW,** Lothian    6,000    E.C. Wed.
18 m. W. of Edinburgh by A8/M9 exit 3; 20 m. S.E. of Stirling by M9 exit 4/A9.

*i* Vennel Car Park (050 684) 4600.

Ancient royal burgh much visited on account of its many historical associations. Linlithgow Loch and immediate surroundings are particularly attractive.

**Linlithgow Palace. D.E.** *Apr. to Sept. 9.30-7 weekdays, 2-4 Sun,; Oct. to Mar. 9.30-4 weekdays, 2-4 Sun.* Dates from 1424. Now roofless remains. Birthplace of James V and Mary, Queen of Scots (1542). See chapel, Great Hall and, in quadrangle, a 16th c. fountain.

**St. Michael's Parish Church** (adjacent to Palace). *All year 10-12, 2-4 weekdays ex. Thurs. 10-12 Sun.* Fire in 1424 destroyed much of the 13th c. church (later rebuilt). Many claim that Medieval building is one of finest in Scotland. Much of the window tracery is exquisite.

**Blackness Castle. D.E.** 4 m. N.E. by B903. *Apr. to Sept. 9.30-7 weekdays, 2-4 Sun. Oct. to Mar. 9.30-4 weekdays, 2-4 Sun.* Dates from 15th c. Formerly a prison for Covenanters. Sometimes called 'Ship' Castle due to its shape.

**The Binns. N.T.S.** 4 m. E. off A904. *Easter to Sept. 2-5.30 daily ex. Fri.* For over 300 years a seat of the Dalyell family. Notable are the ornate ceilings. Royal Scots Greys raised here by Gen. Tam Dalyell in 1681.

**Hopetoun House.** 5 m. E. by M9 exit 2/A904/unclass. road. *May to Sept., daily, 11-5.30.*    Dates from 1699 with later additions by William Adam and his two sons. A splendid mansion normally held to be possibly Scotland's finest. Interior decoration, exquisite furniture and outstanding collection of pictures are principal features. Fine grounds (separate charge) include a nature trail, formal gardens, stables museum, restaurant and gift shop.

**Linlithgow Riding of the Marches.** *June.*

See also TORPHICHEN (Church), FORTH BRIDGES, KINNEIL HOUSE, DALMENY CHURCH.

**LOCHGILPHEAD,** Strathclyde    1,000    E.C. Tues.
83 m. N.W. of Glasgow by A82/A83; 14 m. N. of Tarbert (L. Fyne) by A83. 37 m. S. of Oban by A816.

✉ Colchester Sq. (0546) 2344.

Administrative headquarters of region's Argyll and Bute district. Basically, a rather unattractive place especially at low tide. As a touring centre, there is an abundance of fine scenery and many points of interest in the surrounding area.

**Dunadd Fort. D.E.** 4 m. N.W. off A816. *All reasonable times.* Said to be site of ancient capital of Dalriada (c. 500-850) one of the then four kingdoms of Scotland. Many interesting markings include that of a footprint and bore.

**Crinan Canal.** Runs from Ardrishaig (L. Fyne) to Crinan (Sound of Jura) a distance of 9 m. Built 1793-1801. Pleasant to watch the comings and goings of yachts etc. at Ardrishaig — unless pressed for time and find the bridge on A83 against you!

**Castle Sween. D.E.** 15 m. S.W. by A816/B841/B8025. *All reasonable times.* Dates from 12th (possibly 11th c.). Some interesting remains of what is said to be probably the earliest stone castle in Scotland.

**St. Columba's Cave.** 12 m. S.W. by A83/B8024/unclass. road. Associated with St. Columba's arrival in Scotland although unfounded.

**Knapdale peninsula.** No visitor to Lochgilphead should leave ※ the area without taking in the scenic route by A83/B8024 to Tarbert via Kilberry — some 36 m. but well worth the petrol! Views W. and S.W. to Islay, Jura and Gigha are outstanding.

**Mid Argyll Seafood Festival.** Tarbert (L. Fyne) and other centres in Mid Argyll. *June.*

See also TARBERT, LOCHGAIR, KILMARTIN (Grave slabs) CRINAN.

**LOCHINVER,** Highland    200     E.C. Tues.
99 m. N.W. of Inverness by A9/A832/A835/A837; 55 m. S.W. of Durness by A838/A894 (Ferry)/A837.
✉ Information Centre (057 14) 330.

Small, picturesque village in Assynt district of N.W. Highlands. South-east are the prominent peaks of Canisp (2,779 ft.) and the 'sugar-loaf' Suilven (2,399 ft.). Excellent trout fishing in surrounding lochs. Good sand beaches to N.W.

**Ardvreck Castle.** 11 m. E. by A837. *All times.* Dates from c. 1490. Former stronghold of MacLeods, now a ruin. Marquis of Montrose held captive here prior to execution in Edinburgh.

**Lochinver Highland Gathering.** *August.*

See also ACHMELVICH, STOER, DRUMBEG, ACHIL-TIBUIE.

**LOCH LOMOND,** Strathclyde/Central.

*i* Balloch: Information Centre (37) 53533.

*i* Tarbet: Stuckgowan (030 12) 251.

Most written about, sung about, spoken about stretch of inland water in Britain. A truly beautiful loch 23 m. long by 5 m. broad, dominated in the main by 3,192 ft. Ben Lomond (E. shore) and the slightly lower Bens Vane and Vorlich on the W. Thirty or so islands, some little more than clusters of rock, are confined mainly to the broad S. section. A82 runs the entire length of the W. shore (Balloch-Ardlui) while, on the E. side B837 skirts the L. from Balmaha to Rowardennan (starting point for Ben Lomond climb). 'Maid of the Loch', a paddle steamer based at Balloch, sails up to Ardlui at the northernmost tip or to the attractive little piers at Rowardennan and Inversnaid. Note: steamer service operates *mid-May to mid-Sept. only.*

**Balloch.** Often busy with day trippers from Glasgow and environs. R. Leven has many houseboats, some attractive but most rather shabby. Balloch Park (formerly property of Glasgow Corporation) is a gem and affords glorious views of the loch. The bear park, correctly called **Cameron Loch Lomond,** has interesting wildlife (car or safari coach), an abundance of attractions for children, water ski-ing and much more.

**Luss.** 8 m. N. of Balloch by A82. Many times winner of 'prettiest village in Scotland' title. Don't be misled by the village sign on main road for, if so, you'll have passed through and seen nothing! Fork right at the hotel as you go N. for the delightfully attractive cottages, pier and tiny beach.

**Rossdhu.** 2 m. S of Luss by A82. **See ad for dates and times of opening.** Family home of Clan Colquhoun. A moderately sized Georgian house dating from 1773. Splendid furniture, portraits, etc. Grounds (separate charge) offer magnificent views of Loch Lomond and some of its islands.

**Drymen.** 9 m. N.E. at Balloch by A.811. Attractive village 5
5 m. E. of the Loch of Balmaha. Base for exploring the
Trossachs and lesser-known E. shore of L. Lomond.
Particularly attractive milk bar is just E. of village on main
Aberfoyle/Stirling road (A.811).

**Balmaha.** 13 m. N. of Balloch by A811/B837. An attractive
little spot looking W. across the Loch. Scores of pleasure
craft are moored in a bay sheltered by two fairly large islands.
Good boat hiring facilities. Further N. along the lochside is
Rowardennan much visited on account of its being within the
vast Queen Elizabeth Forest Park which embraces Ben
Lomond.

**Luss Highland Games.** *July.*

See also GLEN FRUIN, GLEN LUSS, GLEN DOUGLAS,
ARROCHAR/TARBET.

**LOCKERBIE,** Dumf. and Gall.   3,000.  E.C. Tues.
70 m. S.E. of Glasgow by M.74/A.74 (slip road); 12 m. E. of
Dumfries by A.709.

*i* High St., (057 62) 2123.

Pleasantly situated town in Annandale. Touring centre.
Local ice rink, used largely for curling, is popular as is
angling for salmon, sea-trout, and trout on nearby R.
Annan. Peculiar pronunciations to some places around —
the hill Qwhytewoollen is, in fact, Whiteween.

**Rammerscales.** 5 m. W. by A.709/B.7020. Georgian manor
house dating back to 1760 with links with Flora Macdonald
(see SKYE) and some Jacobite relics. Works of modern
artists. Fine circular staircase, public rooms and library.
*Early June-mid. Sept., Tues., Thur., 2-5; alt. Suns., 2-5.*

**Lochmaben Castle. D.E.** 3½ m. W. by A.709. Dates from
early 14th c. Now ruin. Robert the Bruce is said to have
stayed here as a boy. *All reasonable times.*

**Castle Loch (Lochmaben).** Adjacent to above. Here is found
the rare vendace fish which is a mere 7'' and has a heart-like
mark on its head. The fish, found also in nearby Mill Loch
and one other, is said to take no bait.

**Gala Week.** Riding of the Marches. *First week June.*

**LOSSIEMOUTH,** Grampian    6,000    E.C. Thurs.
44 m. N.E. of Inverness by A96/A941; 6 m. N. of Elgin by
A941.

*i* Elgin, 17 High St. (6 m. S.) (0343) 3388.

Popular holiday resort on Moray Firth. Excellent sand beach

and many seaside amenities are offered. Nearby is an important R.A.F. station and still closer to the town the famous Gordonstoun School (Duffus village) wherein the Duke of Edinburgh and Prince Charles were educated. Lossiemouth itself was the birthplace of Britain's first Labour Prime Minister, Ramsay MacDonald (1866-1937).

W **Burghead 'Roman' Well. D.E.** 8 m. W. by B9040/B9012. *Apr. to Sept. 9.30-7 weekdays, 2-7 Sun.; Oct. to Mar. 9.30-4 weekdays, 2-4 Sun.* Early Christians are thought to have used this well — a chamber cut in the rock — to carry out baptismal ceremonies. The workmanship was once considered of Roman origin although this is now refuted in favour of Celtic skills. Nearby, is the famous Outward Bound School where would-be mariners are put through their paces in no uncertain terms!

W **Duffus Castle.** 6 m. S.W. by A941/unclass. road. *All reasonable times.* Former stronghold of the Murrays, the now scanty ruins of this 14th c. Castle are noteworthy. A somewhat prominent tower is the most striking feature although the well preserved moat, intact and water-filled, also attracts attention.

**Highland Games (Elgin).** *July.*

See also HOPEMAN, GARMOUTH/KINGSTON, ELGIN.


**MALLAIG,** Highland    1,000    E.C. Wed.
47 m. N.W. of Fort William by A82/A830; 109 m. S.W. of Inverness by A82/A830.

*i* Information Centre (0687) 2170.

Busy fishing and ferry port in Lochaber disrict. Rail terminal of West Highland line, probably most scenic in Britain (from Fort William and S.). Steamer connections to Skye, Rum, Eigg, Muck, Canna, Kyle of Lochalsh and Loch Nevis. Splendid sand beaches to S. notably at Morar and Arisaig. Area greatly associated with Bonnie Prince Charlie.

**White Sands of Morar.** 3 m. S. by A830. A glaringly white stretch of sand fringing an attractive bay. Nearby, on the short R. Morar are the picturesque Falls of Morar while, slightly E. is the 12 m. long L. Morar. The loch, home it is said of another L. Ness-type "monster", runs to a depth of 1,017 ft. and, as such, is the deepest known hollow in Britain.

**Arisaig Highland Games.** *July.*

**Mallaig and Morar Highland Games.** *August.*

See also STRONTIAN, ARDNAMURCHAN PENINSULA.

**MAYBOLE,** Strathclyde    5,000    E.C. Wed.
10 m. S. of Ayr by A77; 12 m. N.E. of Girvan by A77.

A sprawling town on the busy Ayr-Girvan road. Former stronghold of the powerful Kennedy family, the area is now an important agricultural centre of the Carrick district of Strathclyde.

**Crossraguel Abbey. D.E.** 2 m. S.W. by A77. *Apr. to Sept. 9.30-7 weekdays,* 2-7 Sun.; Oct. to Mar. 9.30-4 weekdays, 2-4 *Sun.* Dates from 1244 when used by Cluniac monks. Well preserved ruins notably the gatehouse, dovecot and Abbot's tower.

**Culzean Castle/Country Park. N.T.S.** 6 m. W. by B7023/A719. *Castle open Mar. and Oct. 10-4 daily; Apr. to Sept. 10-6 daily.* Dates mainly from 1777. Considered Robert Adam's finest architectural work. Of the many notable features, the central staircase, the round drawing room and the elaborate plaster ceilings are the most outstanding.

**Country Park.** *Open always (exhibition centre Mar. to Oct. 10-6 daily).* Over 500 acres of woodland park and fine gardens. Exotic trees, cliff-top paths and exquisite seaward views of Arran and Kintyre.

**Souter Johnnie's House. N.T.S.** In Kirkoswald 7 m. S.W. by A77. *Apr. to Sept. 2.30-8 daily.* Burns's famous 'Tam o' Shanter' character (correctly John Davidson) had his home here. Interesting museum with Burnsiana and cobblers tools (Johnnie's trade).

**'Electric' Brae.** 6 m. N.W. by B7023/A719. Here, on A719 an optical illusion makes one think one's car is descending where, in fact, it is actually climbing. Not to worry — it's all brought about by the land contours on each side of the road!

See also STRAITON.


**MELROSE,** Borders    2,000    E.C. Thurs.
37 m. S.E. of Edinburgh by A68; 12 m. N.W. of Jedburgh by A68.

*i* Priorwood (089 682) 2555.

Quiet little town splendidly set near R. Tweed. Steeped in Border history it has a particularly fine ruined Abbey, possibly the best known in Scotland. Ideal centre for touring Scott country.

**Melrose Abbey. D.E.** *Apr. to Sept. 9.30-7 weekdays, 2-7 Sun.; Oct. to Mar. 9.30-4 weekdays, 2-4 Sun.* Founded (1136) by David I for Cistercian monks. Robert the Bruce's heart said to be buried in Abbey grounds. Outstanding features are the

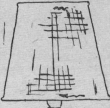

nave and choir. Window tracery (S. trancept) and flamboyant stonework are also worthy of attention. Museum.

※ **Scott's View.** 2 m. E. off B6356. Extensive views over nearby R. Tweed with Eildon Hills beyond. So named on account of its being much loved by the illustrious Sir Walter Scott.

🐘 **Dryburgh Abbey. D.E.** 6 m. S.E. off A68. *Apr. to Sept. 9.30-7 weekdays, 2-7 Sun.; Oct. to Mar. 9.30-4 weekdays, 2-4 Sun.* Dates from 1150. Badly damaged by English forces on three occasions, last being 1544. Refectory, within cloistral buildings, is well preserved. St. Mary's Aisle, wherein is buried Sir Walter Scott and Earl Haig, attracts possibly most attention.

🦌 **Eildon Walk** (E. of town centre). Peaceful 'away from it all' atmosphere in delightful surroundings.

**Melrose Festival.** *June.*

See also EARLSTON, LAUDERDALE, DARNICK (Tower)

**MOFFAT,** Dumf. and Gall.     2,000     E.C. Wed.
34 m. S. of Peebles by A701/B712; 22 m. N.E. of Dumfries by A701.

*i* Churchgate (0683) 20620.

Picturesquely set amid hills and just far enough off the busy A74 Glasgow-Carlisle highway to enable one to forget about the roar of articulated vehicles and the like. Basically a sheep-farming area (see Colvin fountain), the town was once a fairly popular spa on account of a nearby sulphur spring. Good angling centre (R. Annan, Moffat Water, etc.)

🐘 **Moffat Pottery.** (Ladyknowe). See the potter at work. Attractive showroom with craftwork and gifts. Snacks available. *Daily, 9-5.*

🐘 **Moffat Weavers.** Ladyknowe Mill. Tweeds, tartans, knitwear and high quality souvenirs. Clan room. Cafeteria (licensed) for snacks, meals. *Daily, 9-5 throughout summer.*

**Devil's Beef Tub.** 6 m. N. by A701. An extraordinary hollow naturally formed in the hills. Cattle thieves (reivers) used this as a "hideout" in bygone days.

**Grey Mare's Tail. N.T.S.** 12 m. N.E. off A708. Formed by a 200 ft. drop from Tail Burn to Moffat Water. Spectacular waterfall made more so in spate conditions.

🦌 **St. Mary's Loch/Loch of the Lowes.** 20 m. N.E. by A708. A noted beauty spot of S. Scotland. Loch of the Lowes has, where it joins St. Mary's Loch, **Tibbie Shiel's Inn,** a popular meeting-place for Sir Walter Scott, Thomas Carlyle and other great 19th c. writers. James Hogg ("Ettrick Shepherd") the

97

# We are well worth a visit

Every visitor to Scotland knows of our country's reputation for fine quality woollens. We welcome parties and give them an unmissable chance of buying our own and other Scottish manufacturers' products at down-to-earth prices. Tweeds, Tartans, Knitwear and Souvenirs. We are open all summer weekends as well as normal hours. Large car park. Cafeteria.

OPEN ON SUNDAYS

## Moffat Weavers
### LADYKNOWE · MOFFAT
and Shops throughout Scotland

poet-writer who died in 1835, is commemorated by a statue near the famous Inn.

See also ETTRICK (Church), TWEEDSMUIR.

**MONTROSE,** Tayside    10,000    E.C. Wed.
38 m. S.W. of Aberdeen by A92; 30 m. N.E. of Dundee by A92.

*ℓ* 212 High St. (0674) 2000.

Popular holiday resort with all the usual amenities expected of a large seaside town. Fine long beach and sand dunes to break the sometimes chill wind blowing in off the N. Sea. The tidal Montrose Basin leading into the harbour is about 2m. square and lies behind the town. Glens Clova and Esk are within easy reach via A935 to Brechin, thence by B955 and B966 respectively (see Brechin). Montrose Town Hall (18th c.) and Church (both High St.) are the most notable buildings.

**St. Cyrus Nature Reserve.** 4 m. N. off A92. The place for serious botanists or merely amateur plant-lovers.

**Montrose Festival.** *September.*

See also LUNAN BAY, INVERKEILOR, USAN.

**MULL and IONA,** Strathclyde    2,000    E.C. Wed.
Mull: Reached by car ferry Oban-Craignure (45 mins.) Lochaline (Morvern) - Fishnish (5 mins.)

*ℓ* Mull (Tobermory) 48 Main St. (0688) 2182.

**Mull:** Inner Hebridean island lying at approaches to L. Linnhe. Overall length about 30 m. Coastline greatly indented especially on W. Splendid scenery almost throughout, not least Ben More (3,169 ft.). Tobermory, the principal village lies near N.E. tip of island and has steamer connections to Coll, Tiree, Barra and S. Uist. Approx. 140 m. of road are available to motorists. Few good sand beaches apart from Calgary, 11 m. S.W. of Tobermory by B8073.

**Torosay Castle.** 23 m. S.E. of Tobermory by A848/A849. Early Victorian house by architect David Bryce. Castle is only house and garden in private occupation open daily in W. Highlands. Fine family portraits and wildlife pictures. Photographic displays and a century of family scrapbooks. Superb Italian terraced gardens with magnificent views over Firth of Lore to Bens Cruachan and Nevis. *Mid-May to early Oct., 11-5, daily.*

**Duart Castle.** Directions as above, thence 1½ mls. E. by unclass. road. *May to Sept. 10.30-6 Mon./Fri. Also Jul./ Aug. 2.30-6 Sun.* Dates from c. 1250. Ancestral home of Clan

Maclean, the present owner being Lord Maclean. Visitors can see many Maclean relics and an exhibition akin to the Scouting movement. Fine views E. and N. towards Oban and Morvern respectively.

**Old Byre Visitors Centre.** Dervaig, 6 m. S.W. of Tobermory by B.8073. Tableaux of crofting life with narrative in stereo. Tearoom. Gift stall. Craft goods. *May-Sept., 10.30-5, weekdays; Suns., 2-5. Closed Sats.*

**Mull Little Theatre.** Dervaig. Visit the smallest professional theatre in the world. Regular performances. **See locally displayed playbills.**

**Iona:** Passenger ferry Fionnphort (S.W. Mull) — Iona (5 mins. crossing).

For its size (3 m. by 1½ m.) the most visited island in Britain. Dun 1 (332 ft.), the highest point offers magnificent seaward views and, nearby, a delightful shell sand beach faces the little Eilean Cailbe.

**Iona Cathedral.** *All reasonable times.* Dates mainly from 15th/16th c. Original Abbey founded in 563 by St. Columba who, having journeyed from Ireland with 12 of his missionaries, set foot on Iona and so brought Christianity to Scotland. In 597 he was buried here though much later his remains were taken to Kells (Ireland). Island later became a burial place for no fewer than 62 Kings and a number of Chiefs . . . see St. Oran's cemetery, the oldest Christian burial ground in Scotland.

**St. Oran's Chapel.** Built c. 1080 by Queen Margaret. By far the oldest surviving building in Iona. Here lies Scott's "Lord of the Isles".

**Great Cross of Iona (St. Martin's Cross).** Faces the Cathedral. Granite built; almost 15 ft. high and 18 inches broad with elaborate carving. This Celtic cross (c. 10th c.) is regarded as being the finest in Scotland.

Of the restored monastic buildings, the chapter house, refectory and cloister attract most attention.

**Fingal's Cave.** Staffa. 8 m. off W. coast of Mull. Reached by steamer trips from Oban with time ashore (weather permitting). Also from Mull (Ulva Ferry) summer only. Famous for its basaltic columns this great cave measures almost 230 ft. in length by 50 ft. wide at entrance. Maximum height 60 ft. The composer Mendelssohn, on seeing the vast rock formations, was so inspired as to later write his well-known "Hebrides Overture".

**Tobermory Highland Games.** *July.*

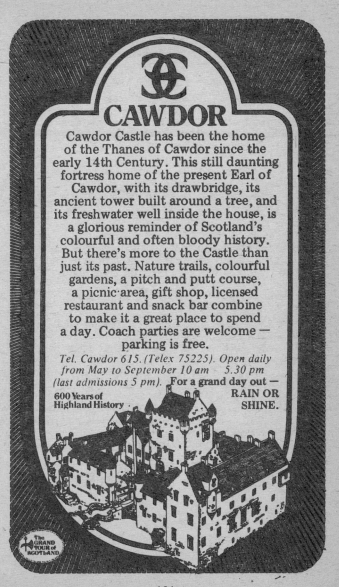

# CAWDOR

Cawdor Castle has been the home of the Thanes of Cawdor since the early 14th Century. This still daunting fortress home of the present Earl of Cawdor, with its drawbridge, its ancient tower built around a tree, and its freshwater well inside the house, is a glorious reminder of Scotland's colourful and often bloody history. But there's more to the Castle than just its past. Nature trails, colourful gardens, a pitch and putt course, a picnic area, gift shop, licensed restaurant and snack bar combine to make it a great place to spend a day. Coach parties are welcome — parking is free.

*Tel. Cawdor 615. (Telex 75225). Open daily from May to September 10 am   5.30 pm (last admissions 5 pm).* For a grand day out —

**600 Years of Highland History**

**RAIN OR SHINE.**

The GRAND TOUR of SCOTLAND.

**Tobermory Regatta.** *August.*

**NAIRN,** Highland       6,000       E.C. Wed.
16 m. N.E. of Inverness by A96; 11 m. S.W. of Forres by
A96.

𝓁 Bus Station, King St. (0667) 2753.

A good town to visit, for a very good reason. Nairn, facing N.
towards the wide Moray Firth, enjoys virtually the highest
levels of sunshine in Scotland and ranks with that achieved in
some of the S. of England coastal resorts. The same goes for
rainfall with Nairn again having a lower annual average than
places like Torquay and Bournemouth. A good selection of
holiday amenities is offered, not least of which are its splendid
sand beaches which extend for miles on either side of the R.
Nairn's estuary. Town also a noted golfing centre.

🐾 **Cawdor Castle.** 5 m. S.W. by B.9090. Home of Thanes of
Cawdor since early 14th c. Cawdor, with its drawbridge,
ancient towner built around a tree and freshwater well inside
the house, a telling reminder of Scotland's colourful history.
Traditionally it was the scene of King Duncan's murder by
Macbeth. Today visitors can enjoy its nature trails, gardens,
pitch and putt course, picnic area, gift shop, licensed
restaurant. *May to Sept., daily, 10-5.30 (last adm. 5).*

🐾 **Ardclach Bell Tower. D.E.** 10 m. S.E. off A939. *Apr. to*
w *Sept. 9.30-7 weekdays, 2-7 Sun; Oct. to Mar. 9.30-4 week-*
*days, 2-4 Sun.* An unusual detached bell tower, probably 17th
c. The tower's bell was used as a means of calling worshippers
⚹ to church. Fine views over nearby R. Findhorn.

**Randolph's Leap.** 12 m. S.W. off B9007. Strictly for those
who like rushing rivers, deep pools and have a head for
heights! Here the R. Findhorn twists its way through a
somewhat precipitous gorge. Don't stray from the path!

**Nairn Golf Week.** *May.*

**Nairn Agricultural Show.** *August.*

**Nairn Highland Games.** *August.*

See also DULSIE BRIDGE, FERNESS, AULDEARN
(Boath dovecote).

**NEWTONMORE,** Highland.   1,000   E.C. Wed.
48 m. S. of Inverness and 42 m. N. of Pitlochry by A.9

𝓁 Perth Road (054 03) 253.

Delightfully situated Speyside resort at junction of A.9
Pitlochry—Inverness and Newtonmore—Fort William
(A.86) roads. Fine views E. to Cairngorms and magnificent

scenery S.W. in Upper Spey. Pony trekking and angling in loch and river.

🐾 **Clan Macpherson Museum.** Treasure of the clan, notably the black changer and charmed sword. Relics of Prince Charles Edward Stuart. *Easter-Sept., 10-1, 2-6, daily ex. Sun.*

See also FESHIE BRIDGE, LOCH LAGGAN.

**NEWTON STEWART,** Dumf. & Gall.   2,000   E.C. Wed.
51 m. W. of Dumfries by A75; 25 m. E. of Stranraer by A75.

*i* Dashwood Sq. (0671) 2431.

Noted angling centre on R. Cree. Picturesque L. Trool set in the heart of the vast Galloway Forest Park (150,000 acres) is easily reached by A714. Equally easily reached is the interesting Machars district to the S. (again via A714).

**Bruce's Stone. N.T.S.** 13 m. N. by A714/unclass. road. *All reasonable times.* At E. end of lovely L. Trool, is a memorial to Robert the Bruce who here was victorious over the English in 1307. The spot is a noted viewpoint. Picnic area and, slightly W., a fine forest walk.

🐾 **Gemrock Museum.** Creetown. 7 m. S.E. by A75. *All year*
w *9.30-6 weekdays, 2-6 Sun.* One of most fascinating museums in the country. Here you can see exhibits of rocks, minerals and gem stones from all corners of the globe. Not only that . . . you will see them being cut, polished and going through a whole series of other processes too.

See also MINNIGAFF, BARGALY GLEN, KIRKCOWAN.

**NORTH BERWICK,** Lothian   4,000   E.C. Thurs.
24 m. N.E. of Edinburgh by A1/A198; 13 m. N.W. of Dunbar by A1/A198.

*i* Quality St. (0620) 2197.

Popular seaside resort dominated by the conical Berwick Law
⚹ (613 ft.), a noted viewpoint. Probably best known as a golfing centre, the town also has a good sand beach and a variety of other holiday attractions.

w **Dirleton Castle. D.E.** 7 m. W. by A198. *Apr. to Sept. 9.30-7 weekdays, 2-7 Sun.; Oct. to Mar. 9.30-4 weekdays, 2-4 Sun.* The Castle, now extremely attractive ruins, dates largely from 13th c. Cromwell's forces demolished the massive keep in 1650. The triple storeyed Renaissance portion can still be seen. Also interesting is a large 16th c. dovecote and a slightly more recent bowling green.

w **Tantallon Castle. D.E.** 3 m. E. by A198. *Apr. to Sept. 9.30-7 weekdays, 2-7 Sun.; Oct. to Mar. 9.30-4 weekdays, 2-4 Sun.*

Dates from c. 14th c. Considerable ruins remain of this former stronghold of the Douglases. The Castle met the same fate as that at Dirleton. Cromwell destroyed it just one year later (1651).

**Bass Rock.** 2 m. N.E. of North Berwick in Firth of Forth. Frequent boat trips (no landings). The 350 ft. high Rock (about 1 m. circumference) is noted for its seabird life, especially the vast number of nesting gannets.

**North Berwick Golf Week.** *July.*

See also DIRLETON, GULLANE, WHITEKIRK (Church), TYNNINGHAME.

**OBAN,** Strathclyde    6,000    E.C. Thurs.
93 m. N.W. of Glasgow by A82/A85; 49 m. S.W. of Fort William by A82/A828/A85.
*l* Argyll Sq. (0631) 3122/3551.

Famous West Highland resort and steamer port for Mull, Coll, Tiree, Barra and S. Uist. Oban rightly prides itself in its magnificent setting on a wide sweeping bay (poor beach) overlooking the offshore islands of Kerrera, Lismore and Mull. Sunsets here are something to savour, not merely for the trigger-happy amateur photographer but, indeed, for anyone with a love for nature at its best. They will not be disappointed. Inland, especially around Taynuilt (12 m. E. by A85), is some of the finest scenery in the Scottish Highlands.

**McCaig's Folly.** *All reasonable times.* Oban's most prominent landmark and one which immediately arouses curiosity from first-time visitors to the town. A local banker built this Collosseum-type structure in 1897 as a memorial to his family. The out-of-character building was never completed though the massive walls with their arched open windows give one an idea of the work undertaken. As a viewpoint the site is unparalleled.

**Oban to Ganavan Bay.** 2 m. N. by unclass. road. A delightful walk from the town centre. The road hugs the shore almost throughout and passes the ruined Dunollie Castle (c. 12th/13th c.), a former stronghold of the McDougalls.

**Dunstaffnage Castle. D.E.** 4 m. N. by A85/unclass. road. W *Apr. to Sept. 9.30-7 weekdays, 2-7 Sun.; Oct. to Mar. 9.30-4 weekdays, 2-4 Sun.* Dates from 13th c. One time home of Campbells of Dunstaffnage and, though unfounded, thought to be an early seat of Scottish government in Dalriada, a kingdom of Scotland. Oddly, the tower-house is of 17th c. date.

**An Cala Gardens.** Easdale. 15 m. S.W. by A816/B844. *Apr.*

*to Sept. 2-6 Thurs.* Delightful gardens in a delightful setting. Fine views seaward to Mull and Garvellachs (Isles of the Sea). On the way you cross the much visited "bridge over the Atlantic" at Clachan.

w **Arduaine Gardens.** 20 m. S.W. off A816. *Apr. to Oct. 9-dusk daily.* Possibly even finer than 'An Cala'. Right on the coast here sheltered by Luing and Shuna islands.

🐿 **Ardchattan Priory. D.E.** 17 m. N.E. by A85/Connel bridge/
🍃 unclass. road. *Open all times.* A Valliscaulian house founded
w by the MacDougalls in 1230. Robert the Bruce held parliament here in 1308. Priory preserves slight remains, notably some interesting stone carvings. Further E. are the attractive gardens of Ardchattan House *(Apr. to Sept.)*.

🍃 **Cruachan Hydro-Electric Scheme.** 15 m. E. by A85/unclass. road. Conducted tours arranged depending on demand (enquire at Visitor Centre). Basically for those with an interest in modern technological skills. For the layman, water is pumped from L. Awe and stored in a huge dam 1,300 ft. up Ben Cruachan. Thereafter, the stored water is used to generate electricity to a wide area controlled by the North of Scotland Hydro-Electric Board. Note: some 6 m. E. of the Hydro plant is the much-photographed 15th c. Kilchurn Castle (no admission) a former stronghold of the Breadalbanes.
**Tours from Oban:** Of the many steamer trips offered (Lismore, Corryvreckan Whirlpool, Colonsay, etc.) that to Mull, Iona and Staffa is by far the most rewarding.

**Connel.** 5 m. N.E. by A.85. Attractive little place near mouth of L. Etive. Former rail bridge (now used by traffic to and from Ballachulish via A.828) is a massive cantilever structure which can be seen for many miles. Beneath the bridge are the **Falls of Lora**, particularly impressive at low spring tides.

**West Highland Yachting Week.** *August.*

**Argyllshire Gathering.** *August.*

See also TAYNUILT, LOCH ETIVE (boat from Taynuilt pier), GLEN LONAN, KILMELFORD (for L. Avich).

**OLD MELDRUM,** Grampian     1,000     E.C. Wed.
18 m. N.W. of Aberdeen by A947; 17 m. S.E. of Turriff by A947.

Pleasant little farming town lying betwixt Ythan and Urie rivers (N. and S.W. respectively). Views of the Formartine and Garioch districts can be had from the nearby Barra Hill (634 ft.) historically important being the site of a battle (1308) between Bruce and Comyn, his defeated rival.

**Pitmedden Garden. N.T.S.** 6 m. E. by A920/B999. *Open*
W *9.30-dusk daily.* Formerly a 17th c. Great Garden created by
Sir Alexander Seton. Passing of years undid majority of
magnificent earlier work and garden had to be re-created,
when National Trust took responsibility in 1952. The pattern
follows that of Seton's original. Formal design outlined in
box hedging with something in order of 30,000 bedding
plants. A garden specialising in heraldic design based on Sir
Alexander's coat of arms is the most colourful single spectacle
at Pitmedden. Quite rare in Scotland are the thunder houses
(a form of summer house) which are located at the W. wall.
The Gardens are said to be at their best in July and August.

**Tolquhon Castle. D.E.** 7 m. E. by A920/B999 (nr. Pitmedden
Garden). *Apr. to Sept. 9.30-7 weekdays, 2-7 Sun.; Oct. to
Mar. 9.30-4 weekdays, 2-4 Sun.* Dates from early 15th c. A
somewhat striking ruin previously a seat of Forbes family.
Many interesting features notably the towers, courtyard and
main gatehouse.

**Haddo House.** 9 m. N.E. by B924 (Methlick) thence B9005
(Ellon Rd.). *Jun. to Sept. 2.30-5 Wed. and Sat.* Present
mansion dates from 1732, the work of Wm. Adam. Home of
Gordons of Haddo, in this and earlier house, for over 500 yrs.
Main features include a splendid interior with particularly
appealing stairways from ground to first floor. Valuable
portraits and antique furniture. Private chapel. Haddo House
Choral Society stage regular productions of operas, etc. in a
delightful theatre near the House.

See also ELLON, NEWBURGH (Sands of Forvie Nature
Reserve), METHLICK, FYVIE.

**ORKNEY ISLANDS,** Orkney      17,000
Reached by car ferry services Scrabster (Thurso) —
Stromness. (2 hrs.) Inter-island ferries from Kirkwall and
Stromness.

*i* Kirkwall: Information Centre (0856) 2856.

*i* Stromness: Pierhead (085 685) 716.

About 70 islands comprise the region of Orkney. Twenty-four
of these are inhabited with Mainland, the principal, having
almost exactly ¾ (12,747) of the entire population. The
islands have a long history and today their inhabitants are
referred to as Orcadians, this name stemming from Roman
times when Orkney was called Orcades. Like Shetland region,
Orkney tends to be somewhat neglected by tourists, travel
agents and other enterprises due possibly to its high cost and
inaccessibility from most large centres. But these islands have
many plus factors. The climate is mild, the summer is virtually

nightless and for anglers and archaeologists, Mainland can have few rivals. Kirkwall (pop. 4,617), the capital of Orkney, is noted for its many fine buildings.

🐦 **St. Magnus Cathedral.** Kirkwall. *Open all year. 9-1, 2-5 weekdays.* Founded 1137. Dedicated to St. Magnus from whom it takes name. Although desecrated by Cromwell's soldiers the building was much later restored and is now the Parish Church. Of its many fine features the Norman architecture attracts probably most attention. Tower affords good views of Kirkwall and surroundings.

🐦 **Bishop's Palace and Earl's Palace. D.E.** Kirkwall. *Apr. to Sept. 9.30-7 weekdays, 2-7 Sun.; Oct. to Mar. 9.30-4 weekdays, 2-4 Sun.* Dates from 13th c. Most visited on account of round tower. Earl's Palace (adjacent), built 1607, is notable for its magnificent Renaissance architecture.

🐦 **Tankerness House Museum.** Kirkwall. *Open all year. 10.30-1, 2-5.30 weekdays.* Formerly a well-to-do Orcadian's mansion (built 1574). Carefully displayed exhibits depict Orkney's lifestyle down the ages. Art gallery.

**Skara Brae. D.E.** 7 m. N. of Stromness by A967/B9056. *Apr. to Sept. 9.30-7 weekdays, 2-7 Sun.; Oct. to Mar. 9.30-4 weekdays, 2-4 Sun.* Remarkable settlement of some nine or ten houses which were buried by sand about 4,000 years ago. Uncovered by storm in 1850. Many interesting Stone Age objects such as beds, fire hearths and cupboards can be clearly seen at this much-visited 'attraction'.

**Maes Howe. D.E.** 10 m. W. of Kirkwall off A965. *Apr. to Sept. 9.30-7 weekdays, 2-7 Sun.; Oct. to Mar. 9.30-4 weekdays, 2-4 Sun.* Huge burial mound possibly of Pictish origin. Inside chamber is considered unique in Western Europe. Many Runic inscriptions on walls of this 36 ft. high Orkney wonder.

**Standing Stones of Stenness. D.E.** 5 m. N.E. of Stromness by A965/B9055. *Open all times.* These famous standing stones form an incomplete circle dating back to c. 1800 BC. Ring of Brogar, slightly W., is an equally fine circle, it being surrounded by a ditch formed between rock.

**Klick Mill. D.E.** 19 m. N.W. of Kirkwall by A965/A966/ B9057. An extremely old (c. 1800) piece of machinery. This horizontal water mill is unique being the last remaining one of its kind of Orkney.

Orkney's Mainland has a number of other interesting sights, 🐦 the most visited of these being the Italian Chapel, built by Italian prisoners-of-war in the early 40's, and reached via A961 from Kirkwall to Lamb Holm. Of the other inhabited islands which are not linked by causeway to Mainland, possibly Hoy offers the most reward. Ferry services from Stromness takes you to Orkney's second largest island where, on Hoy's N.W. coast, you can see such awe-inspiring sights as the "Old Man of Hoy", an almost sheer rock stack rising 450 ft. from a normally pounding sea. N. of the "Old Man" the cliff scenery is probably unequalled in Britain.

**Orkney Sea Angling Festival.** *July.*

**Orkney Regatta.** *August.*

See also (Mainland) STROMNESS, FINSTOWN, BIRSAY. Outwith Mainland: (Westray I.) (ferry from Kirkwall-Pierowall) NOLTLAND CASTLE **(D.E.)**).

**PAISLEY,** Strathclyde     94,000     E.C. Tues.
7 m. W. of Glasgow by M8 exit 8; 16 m. S.E. of Greenock by A8/M8.

A somewhat industrialised town long famed as a thread-producing centre of world importance. The 15th c. Abbey Church and Thomas Coats Memorial Church (1894) are the two most impressive structures. Paisley's environs, especially to the S. (Gleniffer Braes and Uplawmoor) and S.E. (Eaglesham), are particularly attractive. From the first named there are splendid views of the Cowal hills, Ben Lomond and much of the lower Clyde and city of Glasgow.

**Paisley Abbey.** Abbey Close. *All year 10-3 Mon./Thurs./Fri.; 10-12, 1-3 Tues.; 10-1, 2.15-3 Wed. Sat.* Present building dates mainly from mid 15th c. Previously a Cluniac Abbey Church had been founded here in 1163 but was later destroyed by English (1307). The W. front and the nave are probably most worthy of attention. St. Mirren's Chapel (1499) located where one would normally find the S. transept, has some interesting panels and an effigy which is thought to be that of Robert the Bruce's daughter.

**Paisley Museum and Art Galleries.** High St. *All year 10-5 weekdays, 10-8 Tues., 10-6 Sat.* Outstanding collection (about 800) of Paisley shawls. These shawls with their distinctive patterns were woven from about 1805-1875 and during (and for a while after that period) the town became more widely known on their account. Within the building there is also an interesting section dealing with the regional history of Renfrewshire.

**Weaver's Cottage N.T.S.** Kilbarchan. 5 m. W. by A761/unclass. road. *All year 2-7 Tues./Thurs./Sat. (additionally Suns. May/Oct.).* 18th c. Kilbarchan was vastly different from today and was, in fact, an important handloom weaving centre of Renfrewshire. Here you can step into the past by seeing a typical weaver's cottage and the everyday items then being used. Weaving ended in 1940 although the looms are still serviceable to this day.

**Clyde-Muirshiel Regional Park.** 13 m. W. by A737/A760/ B786/unclass. road. 30,000 acres embracing three distinctly different types of park — that's Clyde-Muirshiel. Route described leads one to Muirshiel Country Park 5 m. N.W. of Lochwinnoch village. Its features are a mixture of moorland, woodland and river, pretty little paths, picnic areas and much fine scenery. N.W. of Muirshiel is the Cornalees Bridge Centre (4 m. from Greenock by unclass. road) while at Lochwinnoch itself one finds the Castle Semple Water Park providing a whole range of activities from rowing and canoeing to angling and wildfowling. The Park areas each have an information centre and a ranger service.

See also EAGLESHAM, FENWICK MOOR.

**PEEBLES,** Borders    6,000    E.C. Wed.
23 m. S. of Edinburgh by A703; 18 m. W. of Galashiels by A72.

High St. (0721) 20138. Rosetta Visitor Centre 1 m. N.W. by unclass. road.

County town of Peeblesshire prior to regionalisation in 1974. Enjoys fine setting on R.Tweed and has links with the famous explorer Mungo Park, author John Buchan and the publishers William and Robert Chambers. Made a royal burgh in 1367 by David II. Has interesting Cross Kirk, 13th c. ruin.

**Neidpath Castle.** 1 m. W. by A72. *Easter-mid Oct. 10-1 and 2-6 weekdays, 1-6 Sun.* Dates from early 14th c. A Fraser stronghold, once battered by Cromwell's artillery. Has walls 11 ft. thick. Fine views of Tweed and surroundings.

**Traquair House.** 7 m. S.E. off A.72. Dates back to 10th c. Oldest inhabited house in Scotland with links with Mary, Queen of Scots, and Jacobite risings. Ale, from recipe of Bonnie Prince Charlie's days, brewed here for sale. Craft workshops. Extensive grounds include a stretch of R. Tweed

# VISIT
## Romantic and Mysterious

## *Traquair*

### Scotland's oldest inhabited house

1 mile from Innerleithen, Peeblesshire, 7 miles from Peebles
and a 30 mile drive through beautiful Border country from
Edinburgh.

A real lived-in family home inhabited since the 12th century
by the Kings of Scotland, the Earls of Traquair and their
descendants. It is a home too of lost causes, of adherence to
its religious and political beliefs and to a world which
rejected Bonnie Prince Charlie.
Unaltered for 300 years it tells in its architecture and widely
varied treasures a story of nearly 1000 years of Scottish
political and domestic history.

Open DAILY from Easter Saturday April 5th through to
Sunday October 5th 1.30 - 5.30 p.m. and also in July and
August only from 10.30 a.m. to 5.30 p.m.
Last house admission 5 p.m.
1745 Cottage Tea Room. Gift shop, small antiques and
Bric-a-Brac shop. Craft Workshops in grounds, pottery,
jewellery making, wood working, screen printing and weaving.
Woodland Walks. Picnic area and the unique 18th century
Brew House, the home of Britain's most exclusive Brew,
Traquair House Ale.

*Special events through the summer months: Pipe Band
Displays, Art Exhibitions, Book and Antique Fairs, Craft
Fairs, etc.*
*Trout fishing can be arranged on a private stretch of the
River Tweed.*

**Telephone: INNERLEITHEN 830323**

(fishing can be arranged). *Easter Sat.-Oct 5, daily, 1.30-5.30. July, Aug., 10.30-5.30. Last adm. 5.*

**Dawyck House Gardens.** 8 m. S.W. on B712. *Gardens open Easter-end Sept. 12-5 daily.* Rare trees and shrubs, narcissus, rhododendrons. Woodland walks. See Dawyck Chapel.

**Kailzie Gardens.** 2½ m. S.E. on B7062. *Mar.-Oct. daily* Noteworthy is spring show of snowdrops and daffodils. Herbaceous border and floral beds in walled garden.

**Peebles Beltane Festival.** *June.*

**St. Ronan's Games.** (7 m. E. at Innerleithen). *July.*

See also WALKERBURN, STOBO, INNERLEITHEN.

**PERTH,** Tayside    44,000    E.C. Wed.
21 m. S.W. of Dundee by A85; 27 m. S.E. of Pitlochry by A9.
*i* Marshall Place (0738) 22900/27018.

Steeped in history, this "Fair City" as it is often called, was Scotland's capital until the mid 15th c. Scone Palace, a mere 3 m. N., saw the crowning of several Scottish kings and for many years was home of the famous Stone of Destiny which now lies in Westminster Abbey. Perth is, in the main, a very pleasant place to visit. Possibly its greatest assets are the interesting buildings within the city limits and its two Inches — large open parks fringing the wide, swiftly-flowing Tay. The setting here can be one of rural tranquility, vastly different from the busy A9 "North" road which, in places, is but a stone's throw away.

**St. John's Church.** St. John's St. *All reasonable times.* Dates from 15th/16th c. Best known for sermon on church idolatry preached here by John Knox in 1559. Notable is the vaulting in N. porch. See also Pre-Reformation silver plate.

**Balhousie Castle.** Hay St. off Dunkeld Rd. (A9) *May to Sept.* W *10-12, 2-4.30 Mon./Fri.; Oct. to Apr. closes 1 hr. earlier.* Museum depicts life story of famous Black Watch Regiment.

**Branklyn Gardens. N.T.S.** Dundee Rd. (reached from N. Inch via Moncrieffe Island). *Mar. to Oct. 10-5 weekdays, 2-5 Sun.* The place to go if you're plant or rhododendron-minded.

**Tourist Information Centre.** Marshall Place (N.E. corner of W S.Inch). *June to Sept. 9-8 weekdays, 2-6 Sun.; Oct. to May 9-1, 2-5.15 Mon./Fri. 9-1 Sat.* An Information/Visitor Centre with a difference. Here you can enjoy an audio visual presentation of Perth and surroundings. The unusual building you are in was the original city waterworks and dates from 1832!

111

**Kinnoul Hill.** E. of city centre via Bridgend. A well-known local viewpoint. From the top (729 ft.) one has a fine outlook of the Tay, city and environs.

**Huntingtower Castle. D.E.** 3 m. N.W. off A85. *Apr. to Sept. 9.30-7 weekdays, 2-7 Sun.; Oct. to Mar. 9.30-4 weekdays, 2-4 Sun.* Restored 15th c. building formerly known as Ruthven Castle. James VI visited here when aged 16. The twin towers, some 10 ft. apart, are said to have been once leapt, one to another, by an earl's daughter following a love tangle.

**Scone Palace.** 3 m. N. off A93. *May to Sept. 10-6 weekdays, 2-6 Sun.* Comparatively recent building dating from 1808. Occupies site of former Abbey destroyed by mob in 1559. Many kings were crowned at Scone, the last being Charles II in 1651. The magnificent Palace has outstanding collections of furniture, china and ivories. Extensive well-kept grounds, with pinetum, are, in themselves, worth visiting.

**Abernethy Round Tower. D.E.** 9 m. S.E. by A913. *All reasonable times.* This, and the one at Brechin (q.v.), is the last surviving round tower of such type on Scottish mainland. Dates from 11th c. The 74 ft. high tower is not unlike many found in Ireland.

**Annual Events.** No summary of Perth and its surroundings, however brief, would be acceptable without mentioning the world famous **Bull Sales** held each *Feb. and Oct.* Big money passes here by the raising of a little finger! The **Agricultural Show and Highland Games** take place in *early and mid-August* respectively. **Perth Races:** *Apr., May, Sept., Oct.*

See also METHVEN, BRIDGE OF EARN.

**PETERHEAD,** Grampian   15,000   E.C. Wed.
34 m. N. of Aberdeen by A92/A952; 18 m. S.E. of Fraserburgh by A92/A952.

Important N.E. coast fishing centre with goodish holiday amenities. Sand beaches nearby. Large harbour, formed by natural and artificial breakwaters to N. and S. respectively, is becoming increasingly busy as result of N. Sea oil activities. Red granite buildings predominate in town whose maximum security prison at S. approaches holds some of Scotland's most hardened criminals.

**Arbuthnot Museum.** St. Peter St. *All year 10-12, 2-5 weekdays.* Well presented collection depicting history of town and environs. Other sections show whaling, Arctic exhibits and coins.

**Bullers of Buchan.** 7 m. S. by A952/A975. Huge natural

112

chasm in cliffs. Dimensions measure 200 ft. deep and 50 ft. wide. Teems with seabirds; this vast 'rock amphitheatre' is most spectacular when seen in stormy conditions. The word "Bullers" is thought to originate from the Norman French meaning "boil", later boilers and now Bullers.

w **Slains Castle.** 8m. S. by A952/A975. *All reasonable times.* Dates from 1664 to replace former castle of same name near Collieston 5 m. down coast. Extensive ruins overlook lovely sands of Cruden Bay, itself a noted golf resort. The fragmentary remains of castle were visited by Dr. Johnson and James Boswell in 1773 at which time they also saw the now famous Bullers of Buchan. (see above)

See also OLD DEER (Abbey), LOCH OF STRATHBEG (bird sanctuary).

**PITLOCHRY,** Tayside     2,500     E.C. Thurs.
27 m. N.W. of Perth by A9; 90 m. S.E. of Inverness by A9.
*i* 28 Atholl Rd. (0796) 2215.

Popular Highland resort said, by geographers, to be in exact centre of Scottish mainland. Like Oban, Inverness and Callander it has tweed and tartan-selling shops a-plenty. Good range of accommodation offered. Town's biggest in-season attraction is famous Festival Theatre (est. 1951) which stages plays of high standard both in acting and direction. Many well known tourist spots are within easy reach of town, notably L. Tummel, Pass of Killiecrankie and, still nearer, the charming village of Moulin. **See ad at back.**

**Fish-Pass/Ladder.** Faskally Power Stn. and Dam. (S. end of L. Faskally nr. town.) *All reasonable times.* Here you can watch the salmon passing from R. Tummel (below dam) to L. Faskally. Stages of fish-ladder formed by interlinked tanks (at varying levels), one of which has reinforced windows allowing interior view.

**Queen's View.** L. Tummel. 8 m. N.W. by A9/B8019. Arguably the finest view in Scottish Highlands. E.-W. panorama of L. Tummel and, slightly to S.W. the great mass of Schiehallion (3,547 ft.). Origin of "Queen's" somewhat uncertain although it is known that Mary, Queen of Scots once visited this spot.

**Pass of Killiecrankie. N.T.S.** Visitor Centre. 3 m. N. by A9. Noted beauty spot. Site of famous battle (1689), between King William III's forces and those of victorious James VII, lies 1 m. N. of Pass. The Soldier's Leap is name given to that part of nearby R. Garry in which two huge rocks were leaped one to other by soldier of King William's forces.

113

Further S. on E. side of A9 is 1,300 ft. **Craigower (N.T.S.) a** much visited viewpoint. Given good visibility one can pick out the Glencoe mountains far to the W. and the vast contrasting Lomond Hills of Fife in the S.E.

**Blair Castle.** Blair Atholl. 6 m. N.W. by A9 *Easter weekend, Suns. and Mons. in Apr. then 1st. Sun. May to 2nd Sun. Oct. Hours: 10-6 weekdays, 2-6 Sun.* Dates from 1269. Home of Duke of Atholl. Scottish Baronial style mansion. 32 rooms open for public viewing. Contents include superb collections of china, lace, arms and armour and some particularly interesting Jacobite relics.

**Clan Donnachaidh Museum.** Nr. Struan. 11 m. N.W. by A9. *Apr. to mid-Oct. 10-5.30 weekdays, 2-5.30 Sun.* Most interesting exhibits are those akin to Jacobite rebellions of 1715 and 1745.

**Forest Trails.** Of the many fine walks and forest trails available from Pitlochry, perhaps the most popular and rewarding is that by the W. shore of L. Faskally, thence to its N. end, whereupon one can pick up the Linn of Tummel Trails if an extension is desired.

**Pitlochry Highland Games.** *September.*

See also BLACK SPOUT WATERFALL (S.E. of town), MOULIN AND KIRKMICHAEL (A924), TUMMEL BRIDGE (A9/B8019), LOGIERAIT CHURCH (A9/A827).

**PORTOBELLO,** Lothian (within Edinburgh City boundary).3 m. E. of City Centre by A.1/A.1140.

*i* Edinburgh Tourist Information Centre (031) 226 6591. Portobello Dist. Community Assoc. (031) 669 8275/5902.

Has been a resort for around 200 years. Name derived from Panamanian town, Puerto Bello by George Hamilton who fought there under Admiral Vernon in 1739. By 1790's bathing machines had appeared on the sands to launch bathers into the sea and the resort into fame. "Porty", as it is known, still has Victorian atmosphere but there is also all the fun of the fair.

**Lauder Week.** Held in August in memory of comedian Sir Harry Lauder, born 3 Bridge St., Aug 4, 1870, great minstrel of pawky wit and song.

**PORTPATRICK,** Dumf. and Gall. 500 E.C. Thurs.
8 m. S.W. of Stranraer by A77; 30 m. W. of Newton Stewart by A77/A757/A75.

*i* (Stranraer 8 m.). Port Rodie (0776) 2595.

Attractive little summer resort facing Irish Channel. Interesting

114

harbour was formerly busy departure point for Ireland. Rows of neat, gaily-painted cottages compensate for somewhat poor foreshore. Excellent cliff scenery in vicinity of village.

**Castle Kennedy Gardens.** 11 m. N.E. by A77/A75/unclass. road. Rhododendrons and azaleas combine to give great splash of colour. Walled gardens, woods and lochs complete the picture set against 19th c. Lochinch Castle (no admission).

w **Craigcaffie Castle.** 11 m. N.E. by A77. *All reasonable times.* Dates from 13th c. Unusual in that castle's foundations are thought to have been built on bags of wool due to boggy terrain.

w **Glenluce Abbey.** Glenluce. **D.E.** 13 m. E. by A77/A757/A715/A75/unclass. road. *Apr. to Sept. 9.30-7 weekdays, 2-7 Sun.; Oct. to Mar. 9.30-4 weekdays, 2-4 Sun.* Founded 1192 by Roland, Earl of Galloway. This Cistercian house (ruins) is now mostly visited for its architectural merit although worthy of note is the vaulted chapter-house of c. late 15th c.

**Kirkmadrine Stones. D.E.** Nr. Sandhead. 13 m. S.E. by A77/A716/unclass. road. *All reasonable times.* Inscribed stones possibly of 5th c. origin clearly indicate that early Christian settlement was here or hereabouts. Stones, some bearing Latin words and the Chi-Rho symbol, are among earliest known in Britain.

/ **Ardwell House Gardens,** 14 m. S.E. by A77/A716/unclass. road. *Mar. to Oct. 10-6 weekdays.* Shrubs, rock plants and delightful woodland walks. The spring show of daffodils, rhododendrons and azaleas is particularly fine.

**Port Logan Botanic Garden and Fish Pond.** Route as above to Sandhead thence A716/B7065. Botanic Garden: *Apr. to Sept. 10-5 daily.* Contains exquisite shrubs and sub-tropical plants. Perhaps not surprising as this area rightly claims the mildest conditions in the entire country. **Fish Pond:** *Easter to Sept. 10-12, 2-5.30 daily, except Tues. and Sat.* Remarkable tidal fish pond made more so by tameness of fish, mainly cod, which are fed by hand.

**Stranraer Show.** *July.*

See also DRUMMORE, MULL OF GALLOWAY, ALDOURAN GLEN (A764/B738/B7043), STRANRAER.

**ROTHESAY** (Isle of Bute), Strathclyde   6,500   E.C. Wed. Reached by car ferry services Wemyss Bay (Renfrewshire) — Rothesay (30 mins.) Colintraive (Argyll) — Rhubodach (5 mins.)

*i* The Pier (0700) 2151.

Much visited holiday resort on Firth of Clyde. Attractive sails (especially through the beautiful Kyles of Bute) are offered by Caledonian MacBrayne vessels and (summer only) by the S.S. "Waverley", the last sea-going paddle-steamer in the world. Well organised amenities include golf, indoor swimming, tennis, bowls and, for those otherwise minded, a basically unspoilt island measuring some 15 m. from N. to S. by a maximum of 5 m. wide.

w **Rothesay Castle D.E.** *Apr. to Sept. 9.30-7 weekdays, 2-7 Sun.; Oct. to Mar. 9.30-4 weekdays, 2-4 Sun.* Dates from early 13th c. The now attractive ruin was twice captured by Norse invaders the latter occasion being in 1263 when King Hakon unsuccessfully invaded Scotland. Castle today regarded as one of most important medieval buildings in country. The circular courtyard and water-moat attract great interest as does the Great Hall (see bronze head of Prince of Wales/Duke of Rothesay) and the "Bloody Stair", scene of a vicious stabbing in bygone days.

**St. Mary's Chapel** (at W. approaches to Rothesay). *All reasonable times.* Ruins of late medieval Abbey Church. Worthy of a'tention are two ancient tombs (c. 14th c.) and a pair of interesting stone effigies, one of a founder of the Stewart dynasty the other being Robert the Bruce's daughter, Marjorie. Elsewhere on the island there are many other archaeological remains such as burial urns, stone circles and forts.

**Canada Hill.** E. of town by Serpentine walk, thence golf course to summit. Well worth the short walk from High St. Views of Rothesay Bay, Toward Point, L. Striven and the Cowal hills are quite breathtaking.

w **St. Blane's Chapel. D.E.** 9 m. S. by A845/A844/unclass. road. *All reasonable times.* Built c. 1700. Ruins set in most attractive scenery with fine views of Arran, here only some 6½ m. distant. The foundations of a 6th c. monastery are near the Chapel as too is the Devil's Cauldron, a circular enclosure once used as a place of penance where religious-minded folk crawled round the rugged wall on bare knees!

**Kyles of Bute.** Name given to narrow arm of Firth of Clyde. Lies between Bute Island and Cowal district of Argyll. Scenery throughout this 16 m. stretch of waterway — especially at N. end near Burnt I./L. Riddon — is magnificent by any standard.

See also ETTRICK BAY, PORT BANNATYNE, CRAIGMORE/ASCOG, KILCHATTAN BAY.

**RUM, EIGG and MUCK,** Highland      133 (combined)

116

Three islands forming part of Inner Hebrides. Reached by the Caledonian MacBrayne services from Mallaig (four sailings per week, summer); excursions from Mallaig and Arisaig (5 m. S.) by privately-owned vessels.

(Mallaig). Information Centre (0687) 2170.

**Rum (sometimes Rhum):** Largest of group mentioned. Measures approx. 8 m. by 7 m. and lies slightly over 15 m. W. of Mallaig. Island owned by Nature Conservancy who carry out geological and botanical studies and generally allow visitors to the Kinloch Bay area only. Highest point is Askival (2,659 ft.) near S.E. corner of island.

**Eigg:** Small island (6 m. by 4 m.) some 10 m. W. of Arisaig. Two main features are An Sgurr, a 1,289 ft. extraordinarily shaped mass of basaltic columns visible from miles around and the Singing Sands of Eigg on the island's N.W. coast. Reached from Galmisdale (ferry port) by unclass. road to Cleadale and thence to Bay of Laig these sands are unique in Britain. Strike them with you hand or foot and behold they will sing! Maybe you will be lucky for not always do they "co-operate".

**Muck:** Measures barely 2 m. in length with little harbour at Port Mor to accommodate boat from Eigg. About two dozen hardy islanders live on Muck, a name derived from the Gaelic 'Muic' the sea-pig, otherwise porpoise.

**ST. ANDREWS,** Fife    13,000    E.C. Thurs.
58 m. E. of Stirling by A91; 13 m. S.E. of Dundee by A91/A92; 23 m. N.E. of Kirkcaldy by A915.

*i* South St. (0334) 72021.

One of country's leading holiday resorts and undisputed world centre for golf. Has been referred to as Canterbury of Scotland because of its ecclesiastical background. Two splendid beaches and an infinite variety of amenities. Result — the population increases by almost half as much again during summer.

**The University.** North St./The Scores. Founded 1412. Oldest in Scotland and, in fact, junior only in Britain to Oxford and Cambridge. See 15th c. Church of St. Salvator with impressive tower and octagonal spire. The tomb of Bishop Kennedy, the founder, is here. St. Mary's College, founded in 1537 by Cardinal Beaton, has interesting quadrangle and, nearby, a tree planted by Mary, Queen of Scots.

🦋 **St. Andrews Castle. D.E.** The Scores/Castle St. *Apr. to Sept.* W *9.30-7 weekdays, 2-7 Sun.; Oct. to Mar. 9.30-4 weekdays, 2-4*

*Sun.* Founded in 1200. Was prison of many early Reformers. Cardinal Beaton was murdered here in 1546, his corpse being laid over the battlements for all to see. Within the Castle is the 24 ft. deep Bottle Dungeon and the equally interesting Subterranean Passage.

w **St. Andrews Cathedral. D.E.** North St. (E. end). *Apr. to Sept. 9.30-7 weekdays, 2-7 Sun.; Oct. to Mar. 9.30-4 weekdays, 2-4 Sun.* Dates from 1160 (now ruin). Once was largest cathedral in Scotland. The adjacent St. Regulus' or St. Rule's Church takes the form of a 108 ft. high tower. Excellent panoramic view of the town and its environs. Tom Morris (1821-1908), golfer, is buried nearby.

**Holy Trinity Church.** South St. John Knox, Scottish Reformer, preached his first public sermon here in 1547.

**Blackfriars Chapel.** South St. Dates from 1525, it is all that now remains of a Monastery founded in 1274. Regarded by many as being one of the chief adornments of the town.

**The Pends/West Port. (D.E.)** E. and W. end of South St. Pends: Once a vaulted gatehouse forming main entrance to Priory Precinct (about 14th c.). West Port: a Burgh Gate (built 1589) used as a point for taxing goods in transit.

**Martyrs' Monument.** The Scores. An obelisk which commemorates four Reformers (notably George Wishart leader of the Scottish Reformation) who were burned at the stake between 1528 and 1558.

**Lade Braes.** off Hepburn Gdns. A winding little tree-lined path seemingly going nowhere. Noted beauty spot, it follows the course of the Kinness burn.

**Golf/Putting.** See Royal and Ancient Club House (foot of Golf Pl. near shore). Founded in 1834. the "R and A" is the ruling authority on the game. St. Andrews boasts four full length courses (Old, New, Eden and Jubilee) all of which are open to the public. A nine-hole course for children has recently been laid out at Balgove. "Himalayas" putting green is true to its name with plenty of good (and cheap) fun.

**Craigtoun Park.** 2 m. S.W. by B939. Described as "The Family Playground" this park extends to some 50 acres and its attractions include a Dutch village, Rio Grande miniature railway, mini golf and other amusements.

**Kinkell Ness.** 2 m. S.E. by coastal path. "Rock and Spindle" is a curious mass of basalt rock forming pillars. Said to be the relic of an ancient volcano.

**Lammas Fair.** *Second Mon. and Tues. in Aug.* One of oldest markets in Scotland, now adopts an entirely new mantle . . . that of a flourishing fun-fair.

**Kate Kennedy procession.** *April.* Students from St. Andrews University depict characters in town's history. Colourful floats complete the pageantry.

**Tentsmuir Nature Reserve.** 8 m. N. by A91/A919 and B945. Lies betwixt estuaries of Rivers Eden and Tay. Large area of foreshore, dunes, trees and marsh all of which forms an important breeding ground for migrating birds. Nearby is a Forestry Commission picnic site and several woodland and shore trails.

**Leuchars Church.** 5 m. N.W. by A91/A919. Dates from 12th c. Generally regarded as being one of the best examples of Norman architecture in Scotland, if not Britain itself.

**Leuchars R.A.F. Station.** 5 m. N.W. by A91/A919. The main R.A.F. Station in Scotland. Stages a Battle of Britain air display in Sept.

**Lochty Private Railway.** 13 m. S. by A959 and B940. *June to Sept. 2-5 Sun.* 1½ m. of track on which runs a steam powered passenger train service.

See also STRATHKINNESS (Magus Muir), KEMBACK.

**SALTCOATS,** Strathclyde    15,000    E.C. Wed.
12 m. W. of Kilmarnock by A.71/A.78/A.738; 12 m. S. of Largs by A.78.

*i* (Largs, Pierhead 12 m.) (0475) 673765.

Popular seaside resort facing Irvine Bay. Good sand beach and bathing. Varied entertainments. Name derived from saltworks in 16th c. Ardrossan, which virtually adjoins the town, is steamer port for Arran.

**Magnum Leisure Centre.** Irvine. 7 m. S.E. by A.738/A.78. Claims to be Britain's best, biggest and busiest leisure centre with facilities for all the family. Swimming pools, ice skating, games halls, bowls, sauna/solarium, cafeteria, bars, cinema, theatre. *All year ex. Xmas Day, New Year Day, 9 a.m. - 11 p.m.*

**Stevenston Sands.** 2 m. S.W. Scotland's first nudist beach opened by Cunninghame District Council in 1979. Who said that in Scotland the only way of telling it's summer is because the rain's that bit warmer!

**SELKIRK,** Borders    5,500    E.C. Thurs.
21 m. S.E. of Peebles by A72/A707; 12 m. N. of Hawick by A7.

*i* Marketplace (0750) 20054.

Busy, semi-industrial town on Ettrick Water. With Hawick

and Galashiels forms the nucleus of Border tweed-manufac-
turing. Mungo Park (1771-1806) the famous explorer was
born near here and is commemorated by statue in High St.
Much splendid scenery surrounds Selkirk not least that in the
charming Ettrick and Yarrow Valleys W. and S.W. of the
town.

🐝 **Museum of Ironmongery** (Halliwell's House) off Market
w place. *All year 10-5 weekdays (ex. Thurs.); 10-1 Thurs.* Well
displayed exhibits of old ironmongery form somewhat unique
collection.

🐝 **Bowhill House.** 3 m. W. by A708/unclass. road. *Late Apr. to
early Oct. 2-6 daily (also Easter).* 18th/19th c. house set amid
splendid scenery. Bowhill is property of His Grace the Duke
of Buccleuch and formerly Border home of Scotts of
Buccleuch. For public view there is an outstanding collection
of paintings including a Leonardo and works by Guardis,
Canaletto, Claudes, Gainsborough. Porcelain and exquisite
🏃 French furniture are notable. Fine grounds. Adventure wood-
∕ land play area. Nature trails. Riding and Pony trekking.
Newark Castle (15th c.), 1 m. W. of Bowhill, was visited by
Sir Walter Scott and Wordsworth. Its courtyard was scene of
a callous shooting in 1645 of some 100 prisoners captured at
the Battle of Philiphaugh where General Leslie outfought
Montrose. Permission to view the Castle can be obtained by
contacting Buccleuch Estates Ltd. at Bowhill. (Tel. (0750)
20732).

**Yarrow Kirk.** 9 m. W. by A708. Set in possibly finest of all
Border scenery. Sir Walter Scott's great-grandfather was
minister here and area was well known to Scott, Wordsworth
and James Hogg, the 'Ettrick Shepherd'. Records indicate
that this little church is almost 340 yrs. old.

**Selkirk Common Riding.** *June.*

See also BROADMEADOWS, ETTRICK BRIDGE END.


**SHETLAND ISLANDS,** Shetland      17,000.
Reached by car ferry services Aberdeen-Lerwick (overnight).
Inter-island ferries from Mainland.

ℓ Lerwick, Alexandra Wharf (0595) 3434.

Approximately 100 islands of which less than 20 are inhabited
form Scotland's most northerly Region, a region known prior
to 1975 as Zetland county. Some 60 miles of waterway
separates Orkney from Sumburgh Head, Shetland's southern
extremity and equidistant is little Fair Isle famous the world
over for its intricately designed woollen knitwear. The
"Viking Isles", as Shetland is sometimes known — they lie

almost as near Norway as to the Scottish mainland — formed part of the Norse Empire as recently as the 15th c. and the Shetlands of today retain much of this heritage in their culture, dialect and way of life. Times however are changing and changing rapidly. Until recently these Islands did not rank highly as a Scottish economic force apart from their long-standing fishing industry. This year no less than 30% of Britain's oil is due to come ashore! For the holidaymaker, Shetland has much to offer. The islands are not geared to meet the needs of some though for many they are adventure, discovery and tranquillity personified. Like Orkney, the principal island is called Mainland which again, like its namesake, has almost exactly ¾ (12,944) of the entire population. Lerwick, the busy capital, has slightly over 6,000 inhabitants.

**Shetland Museum.** Lerwick. *All year. 10-1, 2.30-5 weekdays, (additionally 6-8 Mon. Wed. and Fri.).* Depicts the life of the Shetlander from earliest times to present day. Interesting w exhibits on archaeology, textiles and shipping are also shown.

**Fort Charlotte.** Lerwick. *Apr. to Sept. 9.30-7 weekdays, 2-7* w *Sun.; Oct. to Mar. 9.30-4 weekdays, 2-4 Sun.* Built 1653. Well preserved fortification once burned by Dutch (1673) but later repaired. Gun ports are directed seawards, the fort having been designed to protect the offshore Sound of Bressay. The name 'Charlotte' is derived from George III's Queen.

w **Clickhimin Broch. D.E.** Clickhimin Loch. ¾ m. S.W. of Lerwick by A970. *Apr. to Sept. 9.30-7 weekdays, 2-7 Sun.; Oct. to Mar. 9.30-4 weekdays, 2-4 Sun.* A broch (ancient dry-built circular castle with galleries in wall), like others found in N. of Scotland, once inhabited during early Iron Age. That at Clickhimin is a particularly fine specimen.

**Agricultural Museum.** Veensgarth. 5 m. N.W. of Lerwick by w A970/A971. *All year 9-1, 2-5, 6-9 daily.* Exhibits farming and fishing implements with emphasis on olden days. Domestic items (cookery, etc.) are also displayed in thoughtful fashion.

w **Scalloway Castle. D.E.** Scalloway. 6 m. W. of Lerwick by A970/B9078/A970. *Apr. to Sept. 9.30-7 weekdays, 2-7 Sun.; Oct. to Mar. 9.30-4 weekdays, 2-4 Sun.* (c. 1600). Built by the evil Earl Patrick Stewart, notorious for his cruelty to the local crofters, etc. Stewart, 2nd Earl of Orkney was executed in 1615 after which time Castle, one of Mainland's most conspicuous landmarks, fell into disrepair. Scalloway was formerly capital of Shetland.

w **Mousa Broch. D.E.** On uninhabited Mousa Isle reached by hired boat from Leebotten, 12 m. S. of Lerwick by A970/ unclass. road. *Apr. to Sept. 9.30-7 weekdays, 2-7 Sun.; Oct. to Mar. 9.30-4 weekdays, 2-4 Sun.* This broch (fortified tower) stands over 40 ft. high and is generally regarded as being the finest specimen remaining anywhere. Like that at Clickhimin (see above) it dates back to early Iron Age.

**Voe Croft Museum,** Southvoe. 24 m. S. of Lerwick by A970/ unclass. road. *May to Sept. 10-1, 2-5 daily ex. Mon.* Fully restored 19th c. croft house with various outbuildings of period. Interesting old furniture/furnishings and watermill are on view.

**Jarlshof. D.E.** 27 m. S. of Lerwick by A970. *Apr. to Sept. 9.30-7 weekdays, 2-7 Sun.; Oct. to Mar. 9.30-4 weekdays, 2-4 Sun.* The top priority for every visitor to Shetland. The contradiction in time could not be greater for this famous archaeological site is literally within a few hundred yards of the modern control tower of Shetland's Sumburgh airport! Jarlshof, probably the most remarkable ancient site in Europe, shows settlements of Bronze Age, Iron Age and Viking period. It is thought habitation was here about 3,000 years ago . . . some say nearer 4,000!

**Mavis Grind.** 24 m. N.W. of Lerwick by A970. Children will love being here. A 50 yds. wide isthmus is all that separates the Atlantic from the North Sea. A quick dip in each and you'll have done something unique! 8 m. N.E. at Calback Ness is the site of what soon will become Britain's largest oil centre.

**Up-Helly-Aa' Festival.** Lerwick. *January.*

**Sailing Regattas** (various venues). *July and August.*

**Sea Angling Festival.** (Lerwick) *September.*

See also Islands of BRESSAY and NOSS (National Nature Reserve — boat excursions from Lerwick), WALLS, ST. NINIAN'S ISLE (18 m. S. of Lerwick by A970/B9122/ unclass. road), HILLSWICK.


**SKYE,** Highland    7,000.
Reached by car ferry services, Kyle of Lochalsh-Kyleakin (5 mins.) Mallaig-Armadale (30 mins.).

*l* Portree: Meall House (0478) 2137.

*l* Broadford: Information Centre (047 12) 361/463.

Largest island of Inner Hebrides. Overall length about 50 m. Coastline greatly indented especially on N. and W. seaboards thus forming many tidal lochs which, in turn, are fed by numerous rivers and burns, from Skye's interior. The island, noted for its jagged mountain range the "Cuillins", is probably the mos scenically attractive in Scotland. "Misty Isle of Skye" as the phrase runs is not altogether unfounded for

122

this much visited "Winged Isle" as it is also known, has, alas, one of the highest annual averages of rainfall in the country — 1,776 millimetres compared with Dunbar (Lothian) 571! Albeit, Skye is a land of infinite charm, of warm-hearted Gaels and, as hundreds will bear witness to each year, a place which, once seen, is generally re-visited.

Note: In the following text, mileages are shown from Broadford or Portree depending on their proximity to the points of interest mentioned. The latter is the island's capital.

W **Knock Castle D.E.** nr Teangue. 12 m. S. of Broadford off A851. *All reasonable times.* Dates from 15th c. Remains of former MacDonald stronghold once besieged by MacLeods. Situated in the Sleat ('Garden of Skye') district of the island, ✳ there are particularly fine views of the remote mountains of Knoydart on the Scottish mainland. 6 m. W. by unclass. road which crosses the Sleat peninsula is Dunsgiath Castle 15th c. (open all reasonable times), another ancient MacDonald stronghold.

**Castle Moil D.E.** nr. Kyleakin ferry. 9 m. E. of Broadford by A850. *All reasonable times.* Ruins of 15th c. castle sometimes referred to as "Saucy Mary". Legend has it that this character — a Danish princess — laid a chain across the narrow strait of Kyle Akin and allowed no boat to pass without a toll charge! Former MacKinnon stronghold.

🦫 **Armadale Castle.** (Sleat). 18 m. S. of Broadford by A.851. Clan Donald Centre is set in woodland gardens overlooking Sound of Sleat. Museum highlights the Macdonalds. Craft and book shop. Restaurant. Castle is but 10 mins walk from car ferry linking Armadale with Mallaig. *Mid-Apr. to end Oct., 10-5.30, Mon.-Sat.; July-Aug., 10-8, Suns. 2-5.30.*

**Cuillin Hills.** Best approached from Glenbrittle. 24 m. S. of Portree by A850/A863/B8009/unclass. road. Several of these "hills" are over 3,000 ft. in height and, because of their extremely rugged features, require the utmost skill from those attempting them. Suffice to say that they offer Britain's best, but most difficult, rock-climbing.

🦫 **Dunvegan Castle.** 22 m. W. of Portree by A850. *Late Mar. to May (and Oct.) 2-5 weekdays; June to Sept. 10.30-5 weekdays.* Dates from 13th c. Seat of Chiefs of Clan MacLeod. Claims to be one of oldest inhabited castles in Scotland. The Fairy Flag, possibly the principal object of interest, is said to summon relief to a MacLeod chief or his clanspeople when it is waved. Three times in all would the flag waving be acknowledged . . . twice it has been used! So the story goes. Other valuable treasures worth seeing include Rory More's drinking horn, a Communion Cup in fine silver,

relics akin to Prince Charles Edward and interesting letters from Sir Walter Scott and Dr. Johnson, once guests of the MacLeods at Dunvegan.

**Colbost Black House.** 28 m. W. of Portree by A850/B884. *Apr. to Sept. 10-6 weekdays.* An authentic Highland cottage built of unmortared stones. Formerly used by crofters in Skye and many Hebridean islands. Examples of their furniture (also illicit whisky still) are shown. Glendale, a tiny community 4 m. further W. by B884 has an interesting old watermill which, it is claimed, dates back to about 1875.

**The Storr/Old Man of Storr.** 8 m. N. of Portree by A855 thence walk 1½ m. and 1 m. W. respectively. The Storr: A 2,360 ft. high amalgam of pinnacles and crags, many of which are precipitous. Best approached by prospective climbers from far end of L. Leatham thence bearing left. The 3-4 hour climb to Storr summit rewards one with magnificent views of the Cuillin Hills (S.), Outer Hebrides (W.) and the lonely heights of the Applecross peninsula (E.). Old Man of Storr: a detached pinnacle of rock (160 ft.) slightly E. of the Storr and therefore nearer A855. First climbed 1955, it is also known as the Needle Rock.

**Kilt Rock.** 17 m. N. of Portree by A855. Well known rock formation embodied in cliffs. So named on account of bands in strata being both horizontal and vertical thus resembling the pleats of a kilt. Understandably, the "Kilt" is best seen from a boat.

**Quiraing.** 19 m. N. of Portree by A855 thence inland from road at Staffin Bay. Possibly Skye's most notable rock mass. The "Needle", "Table" and "Prison" form this conglomeration of cliffs and pinnacles. Meall na Suiramach (1779 ft.) is the highest point. Superb views, notably E. to the Torridon mountains flanking L. Maree.

**Kilmuir Cottage Museum.** 20 m. N.W. of Portree by A850/A856/unclass. road. *Mid May to end Sept. 9-6 weekdays.* Interesting little museum displaying various household items, farming implements, etc. formerly used by Skye crofters. Nearby is the memorial to Flora MacDonald (1727-90) who made her name in Scottish history after agreeing to help in the escape of Prince Charles Edward following his flight from Culloden in 1745. (see Uist).

**Skye Agricultural Show.** Portree. *July.*

**Skye Highland Games.** *August.*

See also FLODIGARRY, ELGOL, LOCHS SCAVAIG and CORUISK (boat from Elgol).


**STIRLING,** Central     30,000     E.C. Wed.
26 m. N.E. of Glasgow by A80/M80; 37 m. N.W of Edinburgh by A8/M9.

*i* Dumbarton Rd. (0786) 5019.

Gateway to Highlands. This solidly built town has pleasant surroundings to N. and W. Steeped in history it has thankfully preserved an old-world charm in many of its streets and narrow lanes (vennels).

**Stirling Castle.** *Apr. May, Sept. 9.30-6.15 weekdays. 11-6 Sun. Jun.-Aug. 9.30-8 weekdays, 11-7 Sun. Oct.-Mar. 9.30-4 weekdays; 1-4 Sun.* Parts of Castle date back 500 years. Many Kings stayed here, notably James VI. James II and V born in

Royal apartments. See 15th c. hall, gatehouse, Chapel Royal and other buildings. Setting of Alec Guinness/John Mills film "Tunes of Glory". Magnificent views W. and N. embrace Bens Lomond, Venue, Ledi and Vorlich.

**Mar's Wark.** Castle Wynd. *All times.* Remains of magnificent Renaissance palace built 1570-72. James VI and his Queen lived here. Sculpture and rhyming inscriptions worthy of note.

**Church of the Holy Rude.** Castle Wynd. *All reasonable times.* Saw James VI's coronation in 1567 with sermon preached by John Knox. Mary, Queen of Scots crowned here in 1543.

**Stirling Auld Brig.** Crosses R. Forth near A9 exit to Bridge of Allan. Dates from c. 1400. Battle of Stirling Bridge (1297). Nine Scottish Kings from James I to Charles II have used these mediaeval arches.

**Cambuskenneth Abbey.** Off South Street. Founded 1147. 14th c. detached tower worth climbing for view. James III and his Queen buried before high altar in 1488. Scottish Parliament held here, under Bruce, in 1326.

**Wallace Monument.** 1½ m. N.E. off A997. *Nov.-Jan. 10-4 daily; Feb. and Oct. 10-5; Mar. and Sept. 10-6; Apr. and Aug. 10-7; May-Jul. 10-8.* Built 1869 in honour of Sir William Wallace. 246 steps to the top of this striking 220 ft. Tower — after climbing Abbey Craig (362 ft.) by twisting path! Wallace's two-handed sword is here as are portrait busts of Robert the Bruce, Adam Smith, Thomas Carlyle, Robert Burns and others. Magnificent views over Carse of Stirling and Links of Forth.

**Argyll's Lodging.** Castle Wynd. Opp. Mar's Wark. Built in 1630 this mansion has housed many famous guests notably Charles II, James VII and Duke of Cumberland. Many years a military hospital, now a youth hostel.

**Scotland's Safari Park.** 5 m. N.W. by A.84. Scotland's first safari park. Drive through by car and get a close up look at lions, tigers, giraffes and many other wild animals. Boat safari, pets corner, amusements and aquatic animal show. Licensed restaurant. *Mid-Mar. to late Oct., daily, from 10.*

**Broad Street.** Off Castle Wynd. Has many buildings of architectural/historical merit. See Mercat Cross, Tolbooth and Stirling Gallery (arts and crafts).

**Bannockburn Monument.** 3 m. S.E. off A9. *Apr.-mid-Oct. 10-6 weekdays. July and Aug. 10-7 weekdays, 11-7 Sun.* Monument marks spot where Bruce raised standard before Battle (1314). Field of Bannockburn lies some way to E. Audio-visual displays of Scotland's Wars of Independence in

# The chimps are champs

## at Scotland's Safari Park

There's a whole world of wildlife at Scotland's Safari Park. There are giant giraffes, terrific tigers, exotic cattle, aquatic mammals, a happy hippo . . . and, of course, the champion chimps!

Drive through Scotland's Safari Park, take a boat trip and see the amusement park.

You'll feel a thousand miles away.

Open every day at 10 am from 22 March - 26th October.

**SCOTLAND'S SAFARI PARK**
**Blair Drummond, Near Stirling**
(Off the A84 Exit 10 of the M9)
Telephone Doune 456

🐘 Visitor Centre. See equestrian statue of Robert the Bruce.

🐘 **Landmark Visitor Centre.** Castle Esplanade. *Open all year 9-*
w *5.* Theatre with intersting audio-visual presentation of
Stirling's past history over some 700 years.

**Antonine Wall. D.E.** 12 m. S. by A872 near Bonnybridge.
Remains still evident here. Built A.D. 138-143. Wall stretched
from Clyde (Old Kilpatrick) to Forth (near Bo'ness).

**Stirling Festival.** Fortnight's festival of Music, Drama and
Arts. *Annually (May).*

See also BRIDGE OF ALLAN, MENSTRIE, DOLLAR,
CLACKMANNAN.

**STONEHAVEN,** Grampian      5,000      E.C. Wed.
15 m. S. of Aberdeen by A92; 23 m. N.E. of Montrose by
A92.

*i* The Square (0569) 62806.

Popular holiday resort on Scotland's N.E. coast. Many
amenities including golf, tennis and open air swimming pool.
Somewhat poor beach is compensated by pretty little harbour
area. In recent years sailing has become one of town's up and
coming tourist attractions. Stonehaven, like many other E.
and N.E. coast resorts (e.g. St. Andrews, Arbroath, Montrose
and Aberdeen), has its roots deep set in Scottish history.

🐘 **Tolbooth Museum.** (at harbour). *June to Sept. 10.30-12.30,*
w *2.30-4.30 Sun. and Wed.; 2.30-4.30 Tues. Thurs./Sat.*
*Remainder of year: weekend opening only.* The 16th c.
Tolbooth was once a storehouse of the Earls Marischal:
following this, a prison wherein were held (c. 1748) local
Episcopal ministers. Exhibits displayed include items of a
fairly general nature.

🐘 **Dunnottar Castle.** 2 m. S off A92. *All year 9-6 weekdays, 2-6*
w *Sun.* Oldest parts (tower and chapel) date from early 13th c.
Wallace seized castle from English in 1297 and later, when
again occupied by English troops, this time under the
command of Balliol, the fortress again fell to the Scots. In
1685 the castle was used as a prison for Covenanters and 167
of them were held in the grim 'Whigs Vault'. Dunnottar is
often regarded as being one of the most impressive ruins in
Scotland, if not Britain. Of special interest is the Drawing
Room, the Gatehouse and the Whig's Vault.

🐘 **Muchalls Castle.** 5 m. N. off A92. *May to Sept. 3-5 Tues. and*
*Sun.* Small 17th c. castle built by Burnetts of Leys. Notable
features are the plaster work ceilings and splendid fireplaces.
Muchalls, a little coastal village reached by unclass. road
bearing right off A92, is worth visiting for hereabouts is

perhaps the finest rock scenery in N.E. Scotland.

**Findon.** 5 m. N.E. of Muchalls by A92/unclass. road. Village, also known as Finnon, gave its name to smoked haddock or "Finnan haddies" a favourite Scots dish (see Scotland's Food Table).

**Arbuthnott Church.** 10 m. S. of Stonehaven by A92/thence off B967. *All reasonable times.* Dates in parts from 1262. This interesting church was Collegiate and has a particularly fine aisle wherein are buried members of the Arbuthnott family.

**Veteran Car Rally.** *June.*

**Sea Angling Festival.** *August.*

See also 'SLUG' ROAD (A857) Stonehaven-Banchory (good views of Cairngorms), RAEDYKES CAMP. 5 m. N.W. off B979 (likely site of Battle of Mons Graupius c. A.D. 85 in which Agricola defeated Galgacus).

**STRATHPEFFER.** Highland   1,000   E.C. Thur.
24 m. N.W. of Inverness by A.9/A.834; 5 m. W. of Dingwall by A.834.

*i* The Square (099 72) 415.

Much loved inland resort. A mineral water spa in 19th c. frequented by European royalty. No pump room now but waters still can be taken. Ben Wyvis (3,429 ft.) is to N. Resort is base from which to explore Black Isle, Sutherland and Wester Ross.

**TAIN,** Highland   2,000   E.C. Thurs.
46 m. N. of Inverness by A9; 15 m. S.E. of Bonar Bridge by A9.

Ancient little town on Dornoch Firth. Fine golf course flanked by splendid sand beach. Tain makes a good base from which to explore Nigg, Fearn and the coastal villages S. of Tarbat Ness.

**St. Duthus Chapel. D.E.** *All reasonable times.* Dates from 11th c. St. Duthus known as 'the godly Bishop of Ross-shire', is said to have been born here. 200 years after his death (1065) his remains were brought from Ireland and buried virtually where he started life. The chapel was twice violated, the second occasion being in 1427 when fire destroyed it. St. Duthus Church (c. 1360) is nearby. Particularly fine stained-glass windows are a feature of this building which was frequently visited by James IV from 1500 to 1512.

**Tolbooth.** Tain. This attractive 17th c. Tolbooth has a conical spire and is probably the town's most conspicuous building.

At no great distance away is the interesting little **Tain Museum** which emphasises the history of the town and its environs.

**Morangie Forest Walks.** 2 m. W. off A9. A nature lover's paradise where you'll see deer, wildcat, etc. and can enjoy an hour or two "away from it all".

**Open Golf Tournament** (Tain). *July.*

See also FEARN, NIGG, BALINTORE/SHANDWICK, PORTMAHOMACK.

**TARBERT** (Loch Fyne), Strathclyde    1,500    E.C. Wed. 38 m. N. of Campbeltown by A83; 13 m. S. of Lochgilphead by A83.

*i* Information Centre (088 02) 429.

Fishing port and sailing centre on E. Loch Tarbert, a little inlet of L. Fyne. Small boat-building is still carried on as a minor industry. West L. Tarbert, 2 m. W. of the town by A83, was, until recently, the departure point for car ferry services to Gigha and Islay. New terminal now sited at Kennacraig, 3 m. further W. The ruined castle (14th c.) overlooking attractive Tarbert bay was occupied by Robert the Bruce, and much later, by James IV.

**Touring:** Kintyre, Knapdale, Gigha, Islay. The little town of Tarbert makes an ideal centre for seeing some of Argyll's finest scenery. Knapdale, a district lying N. of West L. Tarbert and S. of the Crinan Canal, has already been mentioned under Lochgilphead (q.v.). A particularly attractive coast road (B8024) bears N. from A83 near Tarbert golf course. An interesting tour into Kintyre (S. of West Loch Tarbert) is to follow A83 to Whitehouse thence B8001 to Claonaig and Skipness. (ruined 13th c. castle with huge tower and, adjacent, an ancient Church, also ruined). **Gigha:** Peaceful little island lying c. 3 m. W. of Tayinloan from which passenger ferry operates. 6 m. long Gigha (Gaelic means God's island) is best known for the splendid gardens of **Achamore House.** *Apr. to Sept. 10-6 daily.* The island, also reached by certain Caledonian MacBrayne car ferry services from Kennacraig (W.L. Tarbert) is somewhat unique in that it has an astonishingly low rainfall for this part of the country. **Islay:** This popular Hebridean island is just near enough the mainland to allow day trips from Tarbert. Caledonian MacBrayne steamer from Kennacraig-Port Ellen (2 hrs.) with approx. 4 hrs. ashore in which to look around the island's largest village and perhaps even visit one of the nearby whisky distilleries! See also gazetteer entry under ISLAY.)

130

**Tarbert Fair.** *July.*

See also CLACHAN, CLAONAIG — CARRADALE (B842) for views of Arran, GLENBARR (25 m. S.W. of Tarbert by A83).

**THORNHILL,** Dumf. and Gall.     1,500     E.C. Thurs. 15 m. N.W. of Dumfries by A76; 45 m. S.E. of Ayr by A70/A76.

Pleasantly situated on R. Nith this little town is steeped in its historical associations with the Dukes of Queensberry and Buccleuch. The mountain Queensberry (2,285 ft.) dominates Thornhill on the E. and the vast Forest of Ae with its fine walks is easily reached by A76 to Closeburn thence unclass. road.

🐾 **Drumlanrig Castle.** 3 m. N. off A76. *Late Apr. to late Aug. 2-6 daily. (Grounds 12-6 daily).* Home of His Grace the Duke of Buccleuch and Queensberry. 17th c. Castle built of pale pink sandstone. Ruins of Tibber's Castle (1298) destroyed by Robert the Bruce in 1311 can be seen while strolling in delight-ful grounds. Of the many outstanding treasures on view at Drumlanrig possibly the Rembrandt and Holbein paintings excel. Louis XIV furniture, silver, porcelain, etc. are also 🏃 shown. Adventure woodland playground.

🐾 **Durisdeer Church.** Durisdeer. 6 m. N. by A76/A702/unclass. road. *All reasonable times.* The little church dates from 1699 and has several fine monuments to the Queensberry family.

🐾 **Maxwelton House.** (Nr. Moniaive). 6 m. S.W. by A702, thence off B729. *May to Sept. 2.30-5 Wed. and Thurs.* Dates from 14th c. when stronghold of Earls of Glencairn. Now much visited for being birthplace of Annie Laurie subject of the well-known song. Museum show exhibits akin to agri-culture and early domestic life. Pleasant garden.

See also SANQUHAR, WANLOCKHEAD, LEADHILLS, PENPONT.

**THURSO,** Highland     9,000     E.C. Thurs. 131 m. N.E. of Inverness by A9/A882; 20 m. W. of John o'Groats by A836.

*i* Car Park, Riverside (0847) 2371.

Sometimes described as a "grid pattern" town. Thurso, linked historically with the Vikings, has Britain's most northerly rail station and at Scrabster, 1 m. N., is the mainland terminal for car ferry services to Orkney (Stromness) 2 hrs. Steamers (passenger and cars) also leave here for the distant Faeroes and Iceland. Dounreay, 9 m. W.

# MAXWELTON HOUSE

*Nr. Moniaive, Dumfriesshire.*

A stonghold of the Earls of Glencairn in the 14th/15th Century, later the birthplace of Annie Laurie of the famous Scottish ballad. House, garden. chapel, museum of agricultural and early domestic life, and a shop.

Parties may be arranged for, and can be assured of a warm welcome and a very pleasant visit.

*OPEN: MAY TO SEPTEMBER*
*WEDNESDAY AND THURSDAY 2 p.m. to 5 p.m.*
*and the fourth Sunday afternoon in each month.*

3 miles south of Moniaive on B729, 13 miles North west of Dumfries on B729

by A836, has Scotland's first experimental nuclear station (1954) which, in itself, does much to alleviate the employment problem in this part of Caithness.

**St. Peter's Church. D.E.** *All reasonable times.* Present building dates from 17th c. 1862 marked the last service. Originally of 12th or 13th c. the Church is thought to have been built by Gilbert de Moravia, Bishop of Caithness.

**Thurso Museum Library.** *Open weekdays 10-6 (ex. Thurs.* w *and Sat. afternoon 10-1).* Well displayed exhibits of geological and botanical interest. Items bequeathed by Robert Dick, a local baker with love for natural history and the like.

**St. Mary's Chapel. D.E.** 7 m. W. by A836/unclass. road. *All reasonable times.* Dates from c. 12th c. Unusual feature is the extremely low and narrow doorway connecting the chancel with the nave.

**Dounreay Atomic Energy Establishment.** 9 m. W. by A836. *May to Sept. 9-4 weekdays.* Interesting exhibition gives one an insight of work taking place within establishment. The plant itself has a somewhat eye-catching steel sphere which contains the atomic pile.

**Thurso Gala Week/Highland Games.** *July.*

See also DUNNET BAY, MELVICH/BIGHOUSE/PORTS-KERRA.

**TIREE AND COLL,** Strathclyde      1,000
Reached by car ferry services Oban-Scarinish (Tiree) 4¾ hrs. via Coll; Oban-Arinagour (Coll 3¾ hrs.

**Tiree:** A small Hebridean isle measuring some 11 m. in length by 6 m. wide at broadest point. Exceptionally flat and treeless, Tiree is noted for its high levels of sunshine. Several freshwater lochs dot the island which has superb sand beaches, especially at Gott Bay (B8069 from Scarinish). Due to its remarkable fertility Tiree is sometimes tagged the "Granary of the Hebrides".

**Coll:** Lies N.E. of Tiree being separated by only a few miles of water (Gunna Sound). Island measures slightly over 12 m. in length by about 3½ m. wide. Crofting is the chief means of livelihood for the 150 or so Hebrideans who live here. Good sand beaches are feature of island's W. coast. Like neighbouring Tiree, Coll is a paradise for birdwatchers. **Breachacha Castle,** 6½ m. S.W. of Arinagour by B8070/good track, dates from 14th c. and is remarkably well preserved.

133

**TOMINTOUL,** Grampian 308.
14 m. S.E. of Grantown-on-Spey by A939; 28 m. N.W. of
Ballater by A939.

*Information Centre (080 74) 285.*

Highest village (1,160 ft.) in Highlands though not in
Scotland, this distinction being held by Wanlockhead (Dumf.
and Gall.) which has an altitude of 1,380 ft. (see THORN-
HILL). Tomintoul, a noted angling centre and summer
resort, experiences heavy snowfalls during the long winter
months and the notorious Lecht Road from Cockbridge
(A939) is frequently blocked before any other road in the
country. S. are the lofty peaks of the Cairngorms while N. of
the village is Glen Livet, whose name means so much to
connoisseurs of malt whisky!

See also TOMNAVOULIN (Glen Livet), STRATH AVON.

**TONGUE,** Highland 129 E.C. Sat.
64 m W. of John o'Groats by A836; 35 m. N. of Lairg by
A836.

Pleasant little village on Kyle of Tongue, a narrow sea loch
biting 7 m. into Sutherland's N. coast. Good sand beaches
and fishing are offered to visitors seeking some form of
distraction. Ben Loyal (2,504 ft.), one of Sutherland's finest
mountains, dominates the area to the S.

**Strath Naver Museum.** Farr. 15 m. E. by A836/unclass. road.
*June to Sept. 2-5 Mon./Wed./Sat.* All you want to know
about local history of Tongue and surroundings with
emphasis on period prior to 1820.

**Melness.** 6 m. N. by A838/unclass. road. A cluster of houses
forms this little place facing E. to Tongue Bay. Hereabouts
are many pretty sand bays and unusually shaped rocks.
Rabbit Islands, which lie in the entrance to the Kyle, can be
reached by boat hires from Talmine just N. of Melness.
Whiten Head, 7 m. N.W. (access by rough track) is notable
for its caves.

See also BETTYHILL, ALTNAHARRA, STRATH NAVER

**TROON,** Strathclyde 12,000 E.C. Wed.
8 m. N. of Ayr by A.79/B.749; 7 m. S. of Irvine by
A.78/A.759.

*Municipal Buildings, South Beach. (0292) 315131.*

Good beach and varied attractions in pleasant seaside resort.
Five top golf courses and good shops. Sea activities.

**Prestwick Airport.** 5 m. S.E. by B.749/A.79. Watch the

trans-Atlantic jets taking off and landing at this fog-free airport.

**Lady Isle.** 4 m. offshore. Well-known bird sanctuary.

## TROSSACHS, Central.

Possibly Scotland's most visited single area of outstanding scenic beauty combining loch, river, woodland and, seemingly everywhere, heather-clad hills and majestic mountain peaks. Strictly speaking, the Trossachs (meaning "the bristly country") embraces the comparatively small neck of land between Lochs Achray and Katrine. Ben Venue (2,393 ft.) rising to the S.W. of Trossachs Pier on L. Katrine, is said to be Scotland's "glossiest" mountain and in this respect is often likened to the hills of the English Lake District. Trossachs is reached by A84/A821 from Stirling, the route passing Doune, Callander, Loch Vennachar, Brig o' Turk and Loch Achray. Alternatively, A81 from Glasgow meets at A821 at Aberfoyle and continues by the picturesque Duke's Pass. Apart from being an area of superb natural beauty, Trossachs is famous on two other counts. Rob Roy (1671-1734), who has been tagged as Scotland's Robin Hood, carried out much of his cattle-thieving hereabouts and was, in fact, born at Glengyle at the extreme W. tip of L. Katrine. Sir Walter Scott's "Lady of the Lake" and other immortal works are focused on this lovely district which attracts an increasing number of tourists each year from all parts of the world. As already mentioned under Aberfoyle (q.v.), the most popular distraction is the paddle-steamer cruise on "Sir Walter Scott" from Trossachs Pier to Stronachlachar *(summer only)*. This little boat, built in 1900 at Dumbarton, and transported in sections to L. Katrine was there reassembled and has since given valuable almost trouble-free service. Two other alternatives from Trossachs Pier should be highlighted. A road (pedestrians only) skirts the northern shore of L. Katrine passing close to Ellen's Isle (of Scott's "Lady of the Lake") and continues to the Silver Strand, 1 m. in all. Carry on and you will come to Portnellan (7 m.) almost opposite Stronachlachar. Ben A'an (1,500 ft.) and Sron Armailte (1,187 ft.) are both commanding viewpoints and can easily be climbed in about 1-1½ hrs. from Trossachs Hotel.

See also ABERFOYLE, CALLANDER.


**UIST (South), UIST (North) and BENBECULA,** Western Isles   5,105 (combined).
S. Uist reached by car ferry services Oban-Lochboisdale (5½ hrs.). N. Uist (car ferry) Uig (Skye)-Lochmaddy (2 hours.).

Benbecula (no steamer port) is connected to both Uists by causeway.

*ℓ* South Uist. Lochboisdale. (087 84) 286.

*ℓ* North Uist. Lochmaddy. (087 63) 321.

**South Uist** measures some 20 m. from N. to S. and generally about 7 m. from E. to W. Lochboisdale, the principal village has ferry connections with both Oban and Castslebay in Barra the latter being a 1 hr. 40 mins. passage. Also from Lochboisdale is the start of A865 which runs the length of the island, crosses a causeway to Benbecula and continues to Lochmaddy in N. Uist where it meets A867 the only other main road in the three islands. Scenically, S. Uist is not noteworthy although a marked contrast does exist and therefore adds appeal. Magnificent sand beaches are a feature of the W. coast; sea lochs bite into the E. shores which, unlike their counterparts, are backed by some highish hills, notably Beinn Mhor (2,034 ft.). The island, much frequented by anglers on account of its fine trout lochs, was for a time the home of Flora Macdonald (see Skye) and in 1746 was a hiding place for the Young Pretender. From Ludag, 9 m. S. of Lochboisdale by A865/B888, a passenger ferry crosses to Eriskay (½ hr.) and Barra (Eoligarry) in 1 hr. Tiny Eriskay, (3 m. by 1½ m.) was the first landing place in Scotland of the Young Pretender.

**North Uist** comprises several smaller islands the largest populated being Grimsay with almost 200 inhabitants. The coastline is greatly indented on all sides and freshwater lochs are so numerous that there is in fact a greater water than land surface on N. Uist! Like S. Uist, this 12 m. long by 16 m. (E. to W.) wide island is an angler's paradise. Good sand beaches are a feature of the W. coast.

**Benbecula.** Lies betwixt N. and S. Uist being connected to these by the North and South Ford causeways carrying A865. The pattern of coastline is much like its neighbours and good beaches are easily reached from the B892 running N. from Creagorry to Balivanich. The island, whose size is usually expressed as being of "8 m. in diameter" has strong links with Flora Macdonald and the Young Pretender, both of whom crossed to Skye in 1746.


**ULLAPOOL,** Highland  1,000  E.C. Tues. (out of season). 60 m. N.W. of Inverness by A9/A832/A835; 57 m. N.E. of Gairloch by A832/A835.

*ℓ* Information Centre (0854) 2135.

Fishing has long played a major role in the everyday life of Ullapool and, indeed, this busy village was established by the

British Fisheries Industry in 1788. A thriving tourist trade exists, the more so on account of Ullapool having in recent years been made the mainland's car ferry port for Lewis (3 hrs.). Hitherto the much longer crossing to Stornoway was made from Kyle of Lochalsh. Facilities offered include good and safe bathing, fishing (sea and freshwater) and, not least, some of the finest scenery in N.W. Scotland. Ullapool village, picturesquely-set on L. Broom, is extremely attractive in its own right.

**Loch Broom Highland Museum.** *All year 9-1, 2-6 weekdays* W *(ex. Tues. 9-1).* Exhibits items akin to Ullapool and surroundings.

**Falls of Measach. N.T.S.** 12 m. S.E. by A835 at junction with A832. A little bridge gives excellent views of these spectacular falls (150 ft.) which are formed by the Droma river. The gorge, known as Corrieshalloch, is almost 1 m. long and about 200 ft. deep.

**Inverpolly Nature Reserve.** 12 m. N.E. off A835. This 27,000 acres of mountain, moor, wood and cliff is mainly visited for its interesting wildlife. 5 m. further N., where A835 meets A837, the great freshwater lochs of Veyatie, Cam and Urigill offer some of the best trout fishing in N. Scotland.

**Ardmair Bay.** 4 m. N. by A835. Offers possibly the best bathing in the Ullapool area. Spend some time on the shore here with your eyes wide open — it's noted for its beautifully marked pebbles.

**Beinn Ghobhlach** (2,082 ft.): Lies on the peninsula separating Loch Broom from Little L. Broom. Reached by passenger ferry Ullapool-Aultnaharrie, thence rough track. Well worth every foot of the climb. Your reward is a magnificent viewpoint for the whole surrounding country.

**Summer Isles.** A group of sparsely populated islands at entrance to L. Broom. Boat trips from Ullapool are highly popular as are those from Achiltibuie which can be reached by A835 and unclass. road (signposted) via Lochs Lurgain and Baddagyle.

**Ullapool Regatta and Gala Week.** *August.*

**Sea Angling Festival.** *September.*

See also DUNDONNELL, GLEN ACHALL.


**WEMYSS BAY,** Strathclyde      500      E.C. Wed.
32 m. W. of Glasgow by M8/A8/A78 (coast road); 6 m. N. of Largs by A78.

*i* Largs, 6 m. Pierhead (0475) 673765.

Pleasant little village on Firth of Clyde facing Innellan (Argyll). Rail terminal (Glasgow-Wemyss Bay line) and car ferry port for Rothesay (30 mins.). Poorish beach is more than compensated for by magnificent views of Cowal and Bute. Lunderston Bay, 5 m. N. by A78, offers an attractive shore walk and beyond this again is the squat little Cloch Lighthouse, the best known landmark on the Clyde. Inland, by an unclass. road from Inverkip, is the Cornalees Bridge Trail, part of the vast Clyde-Muirshiel Regional Park (see PAISLEY).

See also GOUROCK, LYLE HILL (Greenock), STRATH GRYFE.

**WICK,** Highland      8,000      E.C. Wed.
125 m. N.E. of Inverness by A9; 21 m. S.E. of Thurso by A882; 17 m. S. of John o'Groats by A9.

*i* Whitechapel Road (off High St.) (0955) 2596.

Major North Sea fishing port with rail terminal from Inverness to Thurso line. The town and surrounding area is deeply rooted in Norse tradition. Golf, fishing and a splendid sand beach (at Sinclairs Bay N. of the town) are among the facilities offered to holidaymakers who can also find much of interest around the large harbour area.

**Caithness Glass.** Harrowhill. Watch the various stages of glass making and, when you've seen it all, buy a piece of fine quality Caithness glassware. Expensive, but worth it.

w **Castle of Old Wick. D.E.** 2 m. S. off A9. *All reasonable times.* Dates from 14th c. The now fragmentary ruins were once an important stronghold of the Cheynes and, from 1569 after a siege, the Sutherlands.

w **Castle Sinclair/Castle Girnigoe. D.E.** 3 m. N. by unclass. road at Noss Head. *All times.* These clifftop castles, one time stronghold of the Sinclairs of Caithness, date from 16th and 15th c. respectively. The now scant ruins are said to have been unoccupied for some 300 yrs.

**Brig o' Tram.** (on coast just S. of Castle of Old Wick — see above). An unusual narrow natural bridge connecting the main cliff to an otherwise detached stack. From here and hereabouts the rock scenery is magnificent.

**Wick Gala Week.** *July.*

See also SARCLET (Stack of Ulbster), REISS (Ackergill Tower), KEISS:

**WIGTOWN,** Dumf. and Gall.     1,000     E.C. Wed.
27 m. E. of Stranraer by A75/B733; 7 m. S. of Newton Stewart by A714.

*i* (Newton Stewart), (Dashwood Sq.) (0671) 2431.

Good base from which to explore the interesting Machars peninsula lying betwixt Wigtown and Luce Bays. The area is an early centre of Christianity in Scotland, Whithorn (9 m. S. by A746) being the place of the first Christian mission (AD 397) in the country. A feature of the town is its broad main street.

**"Wigtown Martyrs" Monument.** On the high ground behind Wigtown this monument commemorates Covenanters who were found guilty of attending meetings against the regime. Notable among these were two women, by name Margaret MacLachlan and Margaret Wilson, whose graves can be seen in the ruined old church. The awful circumstances surrounding their death are stark reminders of the punishment meted out in these grim days. Tied to a stake in the R. Bladnoch estuary the unfortunates were left to await drowning by the incoming tide. A stone on the shore marks the site of this grim happening in 1685.

w **Torhouse Stones. D.E.** 3 m. W. off B733. *All reasonable times.* This circle of 19 monoliths, many about 5 ft. high, date from the Bronze Age. Together they form a circle some 60 ft. in diameter.

w **Chapel Finian. D.E.** 12 m. S.W. by A714/B7005/off A747. *All reasonable times.* Dates from c. 10th c. Considered likely that this building was once used by pilgrims journeying to the 10 m. distant Glenluce Abbey.

w **Drumtrodden Stones. D.E.** 10 m. S.W. off A714. *All reasonable times.* Like the Torhouse Stones these date from Bronze Age. Interesting cup and ring markings can be seen on rock face. Some 400 yds. S. are three standing stones of similar period.

w **Barsalloch Fort.** 13 m. S.W. by A714/A747. *All reasonable times.* Remains of Iron Age fort. A wide ditch surrounds and, from Barsalloch Point, there are fine views of Luce Bay.

🐾 **Cruggleton Church.** 10 m. S. by A714/A746/B7052/thence off B7063. *All reasonable times.* This little Norman church retains the chancel arch doors and windows of 12th c. origin. Nearby are the fragmentary remains of Cruggleton Castle, a former stronghold of the Comyns.

w **Whithorn Priory. D.E.** 10 m. S. by A714/A746. *Apr. to Sept. 9.30-7 weekdays, 2-7 Sun.; Oct. to Mar. 9.30-4 weekdays, 2-4 Sun.* Remains of the 12th to 15th c. Priory Church occupy the site where St. Ninian founded the first Christian church in Scotland (AD 397). A fine 17th c. archway "The Pend" contains a carved panel bearing the Royal Arms of Scotland prior to the Union of the Crown.

🐾 **Whithorn Priory Museum.** Route and opening times as w above. Housed within "The Pend", this little museum contains a particularly fine collection of early sculptured monuments, notably the Latinus Stone (5th c.), possibly the oldest of its type in Scotland.

**St. Ninian's Cave. D.E.** 14 m. S. by A714/A746/unclass. road to Kidsdale, thence path to coast (signposted). *All times.* St. Ninian said to have come here for prayer while establishing the first Christian church in Scotland (see Whithorn Priory). Sculptured stones and crosses of early Christian origin can be seen. S.W. of the Cave at Burrow Head are some notable sea-scapes.

**Wigtown Agricultural Show.** *August.*

See also PORT WILLIAM, MOCHRUM KIRK, ISLE OF WHITHORN (St. Ninian's Chapel).

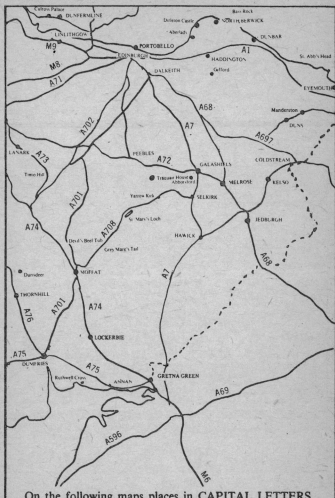

On the following maps places in CAPITAL LETTERS
can be found in the text of the gazetteer. Those in lower
case are generally listed under the name of the nearest
place in capital letters. If in doubt consult the index which
shows under which main entry the smaller places appear
in the editorial.

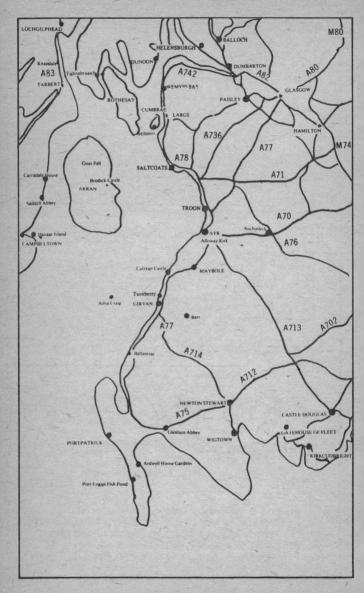

142

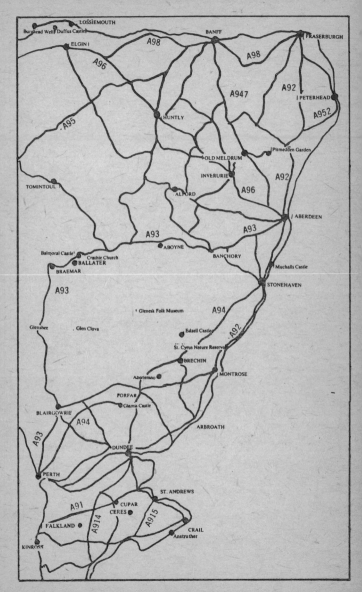

143

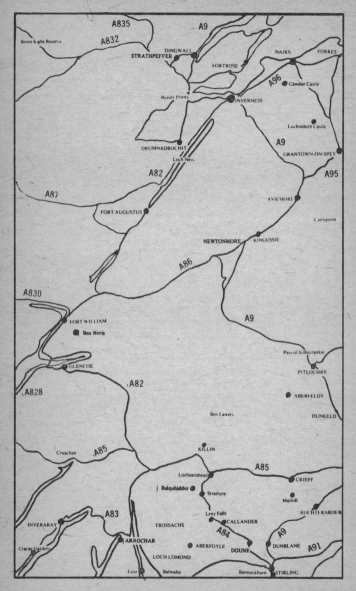

144

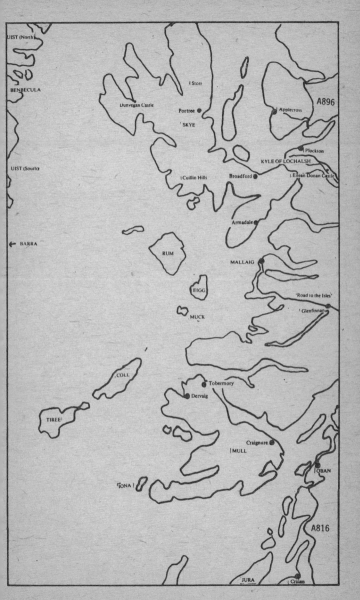

UIST (North)

BENBECULA

Dunvegan Castle

'Storr

A896

Portree

'Applecross

SKYE

Plockton

KYLE OF LOCHALSH

UIST (South)

'Cuillin Hills

Broadford

'Eilean Donan Castle

Armadale

← BARRA

RUM

MALLAIG

EIGG

'Road to the Isles'

MUCK

'Glenfinnan

'COLL

Tobermory

Dervaig

TIREE

Craignure

'MULL

OBAN

IONA

A816

JURA

'Crinan

145

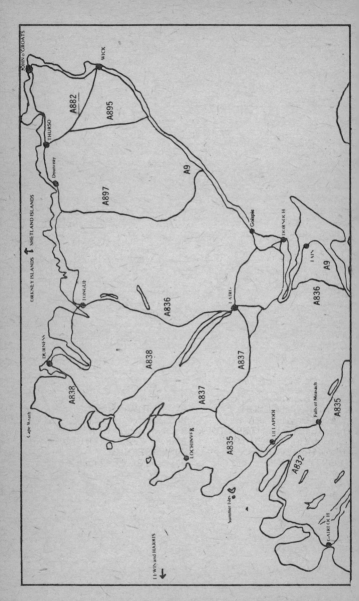

# INDEX

The places in CAPITAL LETTERS appear in the Gazetteer in alphabetical order. Those in lower case can be found under the adjoining place in capital letters.

147

Bruce's Stone NEWTON STEWART
Bullers of Buchan PETERHEAD
Burghead Well LOSSIEMOUTH
Burns Cottage AYR
Burns' House/Nausoleum DUMFRIES
Burns Monument AYR
Burns Monument and Museum (Kilmarnock) AYR

Caerlaverock Castle DUMFRIES
Cairngorm Chairlift AVIEMORE
Caithness Glass WICK
Calderpark Zoo GLASGOW
Caledonian Canal FORT WILLIAM
CALLANDER
Callanish Stones LEWIS and HARRIS
Cambuskenneth Abbey STIRLING
Camera Obscura EDINBURGH
Cameron Loch Lomond BALLOCH
CAMPBELTOWN
Camperdown Park DUNDEE
Canada Hill ROTHESAY
Canongate Tolbooth EDINBURGH
Cape Wrath DURNESS
Cardonness Castle GATEHOUSE of FLEET
Carlyle's Birthplace ANNAN
Carradale House CAMPBELTOWN
Castle Campbell KINROSS
CASTLE DOUGLAS
Castle Fraser INVERURIE
Castle Girnigoe WICK
Castle Kennedy Gardens PORTPATRICK
Castle Loch LOCKERBIE
Castle Menzies ABERFELDY
Castle Moil SKYE
Castle of Old Wick WICK
Castle Sinclair WICK
Castle Sween LOCHGILPHEAD
Cawdor Castle NAIRN
CERES
Chapel Finian WIGTOWN
Church of the Holy Rude STIRLING
Church of St. Monan CRAIL
Clan Donald Centre (Armadale Castle) SKYE

Clan Donnachaidh Museum PITLOCHRY
Clan Macpherson Museum NEWTONMORE
Claypotts Castle DUNDEE
Clickhimin Broch SHETLAND
Cloch Lighthouse WEMYSS BAY
Clyde — Muirshiel Park PAISLEY
Cockle Strand BARRA
Colbost Black House SKYE
Coldingham Priory EYEMOUTH
COLDSTREAM
Coll TIREE and COLL
Commando Memorial FORT WILLIAM
Connel OBAN
Cornalees Bridge Trail LARGS
Corra Linn LANARK
Corryvreckan Whirlpool JURA
Cowan Highland Gathering DUNOON
Craigcaffie Castle PORTPATRICK
Craigievar Castle ALFORD
Craigmillar Castle EDINBURGH
Craignethan Castle LANARK
Craigtown Park ST. ANDREWS
CRAIL
Crarae Gardens INVERARAY
Crathes Castle BANCHORY
Crathie Church BALLATER
Crichton Castle DALKEITH
CRIEFF
Crinan Canal LOCHGILPHEAD
Crookston Castle GLASGOW
Crossraguel Abbey MAYBOLE
Cruachan Hydro Electric Scheme OBAN
Cruggleton Church WIGTOWN
Cuillin Hills SKYE
Culloden Moor INVERNESS
Culross Palace DUNFERMLINE
Culzean Castle MAYBOLE
CUMBRAE
CUPAR

DALKEITH
Davaar Ilsand CAMPBELTOWN
David Livingstone Memorial HAMILTON
David Marshall Lodge ABERFOYLE
Dawyck House Gardens PEEBLES
Delgatie Castle BANFF

148

Devil's Beef Tub MOFFAT
DINGWALL
Dirleton Castle NORTH BERWICK
DORNOCH
DOUNE
Dounreay Atomic Energy
    Establishment THURSO
Drum Castle BANCHORY
Drumlanrig Castle THORNHILL
Drummond Castle Gardens CRIEFF
DRUMNADROCHIT
Drumtrodden Stones WIGTOWN
Dryburgh Abbey MELROSE
Drymen LOCH LOMOND
Duart Castle MULL
Duff House BANFF
Duffus Castle LOSSIEMOUTH
DUMBARTON
DUMFRIES
Dunadd LOCHGILPHEAD
DUNBAR
DUNBLANE
Dun Carloway Broch LEWIS
DUNDEE
Dundrennan Abbey
    KIRKUDBRIGHT
DUNFERMLINE
Dunglass Collegiate Church
    DUNBAR
DUNKELD
Dunmore Hill CRIEFF
Dunottar Castle STONEHAVEN
DUNOON
Dunrobin Castle (Golspie)
    DORNOCH
DUNS
Dunstaffnage Castle OBAN
Dunvegan Castle SKYE
Durisdeer THORNHILL
DURNESS

Earl's Palace ORKNEY
EDINBURGH
Edin's Hall Broch DUNS
Edzell Castle BRECHIN
Eigg, RUM, EIGG and MUCK
Eildon Walk MELROSE
Eilean Donan Castle KYLE of
    LOCHALSH
'Electric' Brae MAYBOLE
ELGIN
Ellisland Farm DUMFRIES
EYEMOUTH

FALKLAND
Falls of Lora OBAN
Falls of Measach ULLAPOOL
Falls of Shin LAIRG
Faskally Fish-Pass PITLOCHRY
Festival Theatre PITLOCHRY
Fife Folk Museum CERES
Fingal's Cave MULL and IONA
Finlarig Castle KILLIN
Fintry Bay CUMBRAE
Fish Market ABERDEEN
Floors Castle KELSO
FORFAR
FORRES
FORT AUGUSTUS
Fort Charlotte SHETLAND
Fort George INVERNESS
FORTROSE
FORT WILLIAM
Foulden Barn DUNS
FRAZERBURGH

GAIRLOCH
GALASHIELS
Ganavan Bay OBAN
GATEHOUSE OF FLEET
Gemrock Museum NEWTON
    STEWART
Georgian House EDINBURGH
Gifford Church HADDINGTON
Gigha TARBERT
GIRVAN
Gladstone Court Museum (Biggar)
    LANARK
Glamis Castle FORFAR
GLASGOW
Gledfield Mill LAIRG
Glenapp Castle Gardens GIRVAN
Glen Aray INVERARARY
Gelnarn Gardens HELENSBURGH
Glen Clova BRECHIN
GLENCOE
Gelnesk Folk Museum BRECHIN
Glenfinnan Monument FORT
    WILLIAM
Glenluce Abbey PORTPATRICK
Glenshee Chairlift Braemar
Globe Inn DUMFRIES
Goat Fell ARRAN
GRANTOWN-ON-SPEY
Great Cross of Iona MULL and
    IONA
Great Glen Exhibition FORT
    AUGUSTUS

GRETNA GREEN
Grey Mare's Tail MOFFAT
HADDINGTON
Haddo House OLD MELDRUM
Haggs Castle GLASGOW
Hailes Castle HADDINGTON
HAMILTON
Harris LEWIS and HARRIS
Harry Lauder (Sir) birthplace
   PORTOBELLO
HAWICK
HELENSBURGH
Henry Bell obelisk
   HELENSBURGH
H.M.S. 'Unicorn' DUNDEE
Hermitage DUNKELD
Hermitage Castle HAWICK
Highland Folk Museum
   KINGUSSIE
'Highland Mary' DUNOON
Highland Wildlife Park
   AVIEMORE
Hillend Ski Centre EDINBURGH
Hill House HELENSBURGH
Hill of Tarvit CUPAR
Hirsel (The) COLDSTREAM
Holy Trinity Church ST.
   ANDREWS
Hopetown House LINLITHGOW
Howff DUNDEE
Hugh Miller's Cottage FORTROSE
Hunterian Museum GLASGOW
Huntingtower Castle PERTH
HUNTLY
Huntly House EDINBURGH

Inchcolm Abbey DUNFERMLINE
Inchmahome Priory ABERFOYLE
Inchnacardoch FORT AUGUSTUS
Interpeffray CRIEFF
INVERARARY
Inveresk Lodge Gardens
   DALKEITH
Inverewe Gardens GAIRLOCH
INVERNESS
Inverpolly Nature Reserve
   ULLAPOOL
Invertrossachs Nature Reserve
   CALLANDER
INVERRURIE
Iona Cathedral MULL and IONA
ISLAY
Italian Chapel ORKNEY

Jail Museum JEDBURGH
James Dun's House ABERDEEN
Jarlshod SHETLAND
JEDBURGH
Jim Clark Museum DUNS
John Knox House EDINBURGH
JOHN o' GROATS
JURA

Kailzie Gardens PEEBLES
Keil CAMPBELTOWN
Keir Gardens DUNBLANE
Kelburn Country Centre LARGS
Kellie Castle ARBROATH
Kellie Castle CRAIL
KELSO
Kildalton Cross ISLAY
Kildrummy Castle ALFORD
KILLIN
Kilmuir Cottage Museum SKYE
Kilt Rock SKYE
Kincorth FORRES
Kind Kyttock's Kitchen
   FALKLAND
King's College ABERDEEN
KINGUSSIE
Kinnoul Hill PERTH
KINROSS
KIRKUDBRIGHT
Kirkmadrine Stones
   PORTPATRICK
Kisimul Castle BARRA
Klick Mill ORKNEY
Knapdale LOCHGILPHEAD
Knock Castle SKYE
KYLE OF LOCHALSH
Kyles of Bute ROTHESAY

Lade Braes ST. ANDREWS
Lady Stair's House EDINBURGH
LAIRG
Lake of Menteith ABERFOYLE
LANARK
Landmark Visitor Centre
   AVIEMORE
Landmark Visitor Centre
   STIRLING
Land o' Burns AYR
LARGS Laurieston Castle
   EDINBURGH
Leith Hall HUNTLY
Leny Falls CALLANDER
Leuchars ST. ANDREWS

LEWIS and HARRIS  
Lincluden College DUMFRIES  
Lindores Abbey CUPAR  
LINLITHGOW  
Little Houses DUNKELD  
Little Theatre MULL and IONA  
Loch-an-Eilean AVIEMORE  
Loch Broom Museum ULLAPOOL  
Lochearnhead KILLIN  
Loch Garten AVIEMORE  
LOCHGILPHEAD  
Lochindorb Castle GRANTOWN-ON-SPEY  
LOCHINVER  
Loch Leven Castle KINROSS  
LOCH LOMOND  
Lochmaben Castle LOCKERBIE  
Lochmaben Stone GRETNA GREEN  
Loch Ness Monster DRUMNA-DROCHIT  
Loch of the Lowes DUNKELD  
Loch of the Lowes MOFFAT  
Lochty Private Railway ST. ANDREWS  
LOCKERBIE  
Lomond Hills FALKLAND  
Lomondside Knitwear BALLOCH  
LOSSIEMOUTH  
LUSS LOCH LOMOND  

McCaig's Folly OBAN  
Machrie Stones ARRAN  
Mac Lellan's Castle KIRKUDBRIGHT  
Maes Howe ORKNEY  
Magnum Leisure Centre (Irvine) SALTCOATS  
'Maid of the Loch' LOCH LOMOND  
MALLAIG  
Manderston DUNS  
Marischal College ABERDEEN  
Mar's Wark STIRLING  
Martyr's Monument ST. ANDREWS  
Martyr's Monument WIGTOWN  
Mary Queen of Scots House JEDBURGH  
Mavi's Grind SHETLAND  
Maxwelton House THORNHILL  
MAYBOLE  
Meigle Museum BLAIRGOWRIE  
Mellerstain KELSO  

Melness TONGUE  
MELROSE  
Mercat Cross CRIEFF  
Midsteeple DUMFRIES  
Millport CUMBRAE  
MOFFAT  
MONTROSE  
Mote of Urr CASTLE DOUGLAS  
Mousa Broch SHETLAND  
Muchalls Castle STONEHAVEN  
Muck RUM, EIGG and MUCK  
Muir of Ord DINGWALL  
MULL and IONA  
Museum of Childhood EDINBURGH  
Museum of Flights HADDINGTON  
Museum of Ironmongery SELKIRK  
Museum of Islay Life ISLAY  
Museum of Scottish Tartans CRIEFF  
Museum of Transport GLASGOW  
Muthill Church CRIEFF  
Myreton Motor Museum HADDINGTON  

NAIRN  
Neidpath Castle PEEBLES  
Nelson Monument FORRES  
Newark Castle SELKIRK  
New Lanark LANARK  
NEWTONMORE  
NEWTON STEWART  
NORTH BERWICK  
North Lorn Folk Museum GLENCOE  

OBAN  
Old Blacksmith's Shop GRETNA GREEN  
Old Byre Visitors Centre MULL and IONA  
Old Man of Hoy ORKNEY  
Old Man of Storr SKYE  
OLD MELDRUM  
Old Steeple DUNDEE  
Orchardton Tower CASTLE DOUGLAS  
ORKNEY ISLANDS  

PAISLEY  
Palace of Holyroodhouse EDINBURGH  
Pass of Killiecrankie PITLOCHRY  
PEEBLES

Pends ST. ANDREWS
People's Palace GLASGOW
PERTH
PETERHEAD
Phantassie Dovecot DUNBAR
Pitcaple Castle INVERURIE
PITLOCHRY
Pitmedden Garden OLD
  MELDRUM
Pittencrieff Park DUNFERMLINE
Plockton KYLE OF LOCHALSH
Pluscarden Abbey ELGIN
Pollok House GLASGOW
Port Logan Fish Pond PORT-
  PATRICK
Portnahaven ISLAY
PORTOBELLO
PORTPATRICK
Portsoy BANFF
Prestongrange DALKEITH
Preston Mill DUNBAR
Prestwick Airport TROON
Princes Street EDINBURGH
Provand's Lordship GLASGOW
Provan Hall GLASGOW
Provost Ross's House ABERDEEN
Provost Skene's House
  ABERDEEN

Queen Elizabeth Forest Park LOCH
  LOMOND
Queen's View PITLOCHRY
Quiraing SKYE

Rammerscales LOCKERBIE
Randolph's Leap NAIRN
'Rest and be Thankful'
  ARROCHAR
Restenneth Priory FORFAR
Rhinns Lighthouse ISLAY
'Road to the Isles' FORT
  WILLIAM
Robinson Crusoe CRAIL
Rob Roy's Grave CALLANDER
Rock and Spindle ST. ANDREWS
Rocmar Gifts ISLAY
Rosemarkie FORTROSE
Rossdhu LOCH LOMOND
Rosslyn Chapel DALKEITH
ROTHESAY
Rowardennan LOCH LOMOND
Royal Botanic Gardens
  EDINBURGH
RUM, EIGG and MUCK

Ruthven Barracks KINGUSSIE
Ruthwell Cross ANNAN

St. Abb's Head EYEMOUTH
ST. ANDREWS
St. Blane's Chapel ROTHESAY
St. Bride's Church LANARK
St. Clement's Church LEWIS and
  HARRIS
St. Columba's Cave
  LOCHGILPHEAD
St. Cyrus Nature Reserve
  MONTROSE
St. Duthus Chapel TAIN
St. Giles High Kirk EDINBURGH
St. John's Church PERTH
St. Machar's Cathedral
  ABERDEEN
St. Magnus Cathedral ORKNEY
St. Mary's Chapel ROTHESAY
St. Mary's Chapel THURSO
St. Mary's Church ABERFELDY
St. Mary's Loch MOFFAT
St. Mary's Pleasance
  HADDINGTON
St. Michael's Church
  LINLITHGOW
St. Ninian's Cave WIGTOWN
St. Oran's Chapel MULL and IONA
St. Peter's Church THURSO
St. Vigean's Museum ARBROATH
Saddell Abbey CAMPBELTOWN
SALTCOATS
Santa Claus Land AVIEMORE
Scalloway Castle SHETLAND
Scone Palace PERTH
Scotland's Safari Park STIRLING
Scotstarvit Tower CUPAR
Scottish Fisheries Museum
  (Anstruther) CRAIL
Scottish Marine Biological Station
  CUMBRAE
Scottish Museum of Wool Textiles
  GALASHIELS
Scott's View MELROSE
SELKIRK
Seton Collegiate Church
  DALKEITH
Shawbost Museum LEWIS and
  HARRIS
Sheriffmuir DUNBLANE
SHETLAND ISLANDS
Signal Tower Museum
  ARBROATH

'Sir Walter Scott' TROSSACHS
Skara Brae ORKNEY
Skelmorlie Aisle LARGS
SKYE
Slains Castle PETERHEAD
Smailholm Tower KELSO
Smoo Caves DURNESS
Souter Johnnie's House MAYBOLE
Spynie Palace ELGIN
Stenness Stones ORKNEY
Stevenston 'nudist' beach
    SALTCOATS
Stewartry Museum
    KIRKUDBRIGHT
STIRLING
STONEHAVEN
Stornoway LEWIS and HARRIS
Storr SKYE
Strathallan Aircraft Collection
    AUCHTERARDER
Strathclyde Regional Park
    HAMILTON
Strathern Glass Works CRIEFF
Strath Naver Museum TONGUE
STRATHPEFFER
Strathspey Railway AVIEMORE
Strathyre CALLANDER
Strone Gardens INVERARAY
Struie Hill DINGWALL
'Study' DUNFERMLINE
Study GLENCOE
Summer Isles ULLAPOOL
Sweetheart Abbey DUMFRIES

TAIN
Tam o' Shanter Inn AYR
Tankerness House ORKNEY
Tantallon Castle NORTH
    BERWICK
TARBERT (Loch Fyne)
Tentsmuir ST. ANDREWS
THORNHILL
Threave Castle CASTLE
    DOUGLAS
THURSO
Tibbie Shiel's Inn MOFFAT
Tighnabruaich DUNOON
Tinto Hill LANARK
TIREE and COLL
Tolbooth CRAIL

Tolbooth TAIN
Tolbooth Museum STONEHAVEN
Toll Inn GRETNA GREEN
Tolquhon Castle OLD MELDRUM
TOMINTOUL
TONGUE
Torhouse Stones WIGTOWN
Torosay Castle MULL and IONA
Traquair House PEEBLES
TROON
TROSSACHS
Tullibardine Chapel
    AUCHTERARDER
Turnberry GIRVAN

UIST (South), UIST (North) and
    BENBECULA
ULLAPOOL
Union Suspension Bridge
    COLDSTREAM
Urquhart Castle
    DRUMNADROCHIT

Visitor Centre GLENCOE
Voe Croft Museum SHETLAND

Wade's Bridge ABERFELDY
Wallace Monument STIRLING
'Waverley' GLASGOW
Wax Museum EDINBURGH
Weaver's Cottage PAISLEY
Wee Museum BANCHORY
WEMYSS BAY
West Highland Museum FORT
    WILLIAM
West Port ST. ANDREWS
White Corries Ski Centre
    GLENCOE
White Sands of Morar MALLAIG
Whithorn Priory WIGTOWN
WICK
WIGTOWN
Winton House HADDINGTON
Witch's Stone DORNOCH
Witch's Stone FORRES

Yarrow Kirk SELKIRK
Yew Tree ABERFELDY
Younger Botanic Gardens
    DUNOON

# DOUNE

### DOUNE MOTOR MUSEUM

Situated 8 miles N/W of Stirling, this converted farm building houses a superb collection of Vintage, Post Vintage & Thoroughbred Motor Cars. Approximately thirty five cars are on display ranging from Alfa Romeos, Hispano Suiza, Jaguars and Bentleys, to the second oldest Rolls Royce in the world. Opening times — Daily from 1st April to 31st October. April and May 10 a.m. - 4.30 p.m., June, July and August 10 a.m. - 6 p.m., Sept. & Oct. 10 a.m. - 4.30 p.m. Admission charged to museum, free car park, toilets and Picnic area. Self service Cafeteria, Tourist Shop, Coaches welcome. Reduction for parties of 20 adults and over.

### DOUNE MOTOR RACING HILL CLIMB

This testing tarmac track, just under one mile in length was built in 1969. It is situated at the Motor Museum and meetings are held three times annually in April, June & September. The meetings are two days Saturday/Sunday and entries range from formula one racing cars, special Saloons, sports and historic racing cars. For times, exact dates, admission charges, etc., see current adverts.

**For Further Particulars contact The Manager, Doune Admissions Ltd., Doune, Perthshire. Tel: Doune 203.**

# EDINBURGH

# LOCH LOMOND

**INVERARY**

# AUCHINDRAIN
## by Inveraray

Open-air museum of life in the past for the ordinary
people of the Highlands, on an original communal-
tenancy farm. Houses, barns, crops, livestock.

*Easter - Sept. 30; Weekdays 10 to 6, Sundays 2 to 6*
*Licensed Restaurant    Car Park*
*Adults 45p, children 20p (1979)*
*Special terms for organised parties. Tel. Furnace 235*

**PITLOCHRY**

# Pitlochry Festival Theatre

**30th Season of DRAMA, MUSIC and ART**
**May 9 to October 4, 1980**

**The Plays:**
FILUMENA (Eduardo de Filippo) * THE UNVARNISHED
TRUTH (Royce Ryton) * THE IMPORTANCE OF BEING
EARNEST (Oscar Wilde) * DINNER WITH THE FAMILY
(Jean Anouilh) * MR. KLEBS AND ROZALIE (René de
Obaldia) British Premiere * DEADLINE (David
Hutchison) World Premiere
7 Celebrity Concerts * Art * Recitals * Puppets
* Plays in Progress * Restaurant
*Send SAE for Prog. & Hotel List.*      *Tel: (0796) 2680*

Visit Scotland's **'THEATRE IN THE HILLS'**

# INDEX TO ADVERTISERS

Thanks to the support of our advertisers we are able to keep down the cost of this guide. We urge you to support them in your travels. The place under which those listed below can be found in CAPITAL LETTERS to the right.

*See the preceding pages.

*There are five guides in the*
# Where to go
# What to do
series...

**S.E. England,** Kent, Surrey, Sussex,
London S. of the Thames — 80p

**South England,** Hants, Dorset, Wilts and the Isle
of Wight — 80p

**S.W. England,** Cornwall, Devon, Somerset and
Avon — 90p

**N.W. England,** Cumbria, Lancs, Cheshire including
the Lake District, Peak District and
Yorkshire Dales — 90p

**Scotland,** — 90p

*In addition there are three guides in the*
# Pubbing, Eating
# & Sleeping
series ...

**S.W. England,** Devon & Cornwall — 90p

**South of England**, Hants, Dorset, Wilts, Isle
of Wight — 60p

**S.E. England,** Kent, Surrey, Sussex — 60p

*From bookshops and newsagents or plus 15p each
for postage and packing from:*
Heritage Publications, Merchants House, Barley
Market Street, Tavistock, Devon.